To c[...]
N[...]
[...]

Best
[signature]
Jne 1997

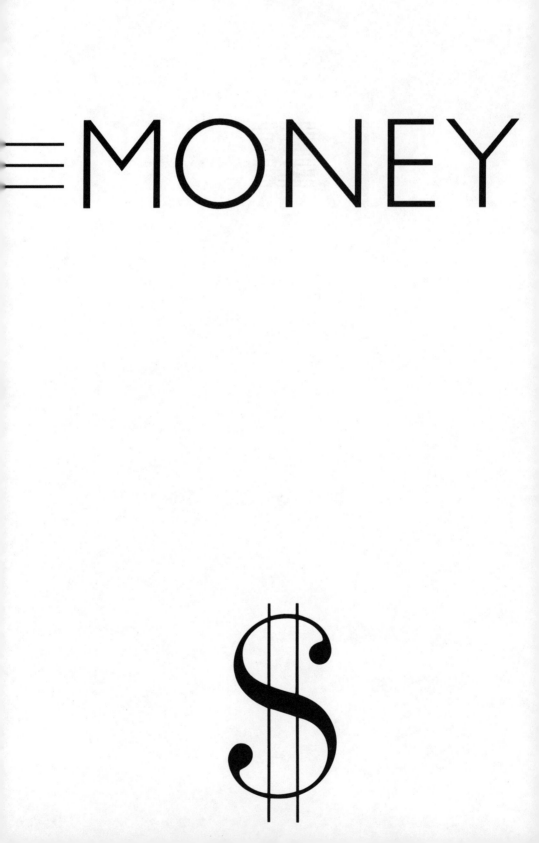

SMART

Secrets Women Need to Know About Money

Esther M. Berger, CFP

FIRST VICE PRESIDENT,

PAINEWEBBER INCORPORATED

WITH CONNIE CHURCH HASBUN

Simon & Schuster

New York   London   Toronto   Sydney   Tokyo   Singapore

SIMON & SCHUSTER
Simon & Schuster Building
Rockefeller Center
1230 Avenue of the Americas
New York, New York 10020

Designed by Liney Li
Manufactured in the United States of America

1   2   3   4   5   6   7   8   9   10

Library of Congress Cataloging in Publication Data

Berger, Esther M.
Money smart : secrets women need to know about money /
by Esther M. Berger : with Connie Church Hasbun.
p.   cm.
1. Women—Finance, Personal.   I. Hasbun, Connie Church.   II. Title.
HG179.B46   1993
332.024'0082—dc20   93-2694
CIP

ISBN: 0-671-76061-0

The opinions expressed herein are solely those of the author and do not necessarily
reflect those of PaineWebber Incorporated or its affiliates. The views expressed
are based on the author's personal experiences and should not be construed
as the norm for all investors.

Acknowledgments

Over the past several years I've had the pleasure and privilege of meeting some of the best and brightest women in America. All have inspired me, and many have become my friends.

My sincere thanks to Nancy Abrams, Nettie Becker, Toni Bernay, Sunny Bernstein, Teri Bialosky, Leah Bishop, Kathleen Brown, Sheri Cannon, Laura Ehrenberg, Beth Fisher, Tracy Gary, Patty Glaser, Sharon Grinage, Jody Hauber, Lyn Hensle, Polina Jaeger, Alice Leichter, Renée Martin, Stacy Phillips, Jayne Shapiro, Rita Sinder, Shirley Stark, Toni Stone, Marge Tabankin, Debre Katz Weintraub, and Peg Yorkin for their wisdom and their support.

Dan Strone at the William Morris Agency brings a new dimension to the word *patience,* and his assistant, Sarah Winer, is a twenty-something muse to a forty-something author. Bob Asahina and Sarah Pinckney at Simon & Schuster are both consummate professionals and awfully nice people.

My assistant, Jerri Gholson, starts every morning with a smile and keeps me smiling.

Debbie Schor has always been and will always be very special to me. Ginnie Knight is way beyond incredible. Joann Hulkower's unfailing generosity consistently knocks my socks off. And Feigie Zilberstein —whatever I could say wouldn't be nearly enough. Thank you.

For my guys, Michael, Jeffrey, and David.
And most of all, for Leon.

CONTENTS

ment Step . . . Packaging Your Warm Fuzzies for Male Consumption . . . Running the Numbers . . . What Inflation Really Means in Terms of Your Warm Fuzzies and Your Real Rate of Return . . . Other People's Warm Fuzzies

The Many Roles Your Money Plays . . . The Three Best Stores in Town: Cash, Stocks, and Bonds . . . Making Your Shopping List . . . Window-Shopping . . . Packaging Your Purchases . . . Shopping for a Mutual Fund . . . Custom Tailoring: Creating Your Own Portfolio . . . You Can't Have It Both Ways . . . Making It Happen . . . Income versus Principal . . . Bread, Butter, and Truffles . . . Using Personal Shoppers . . . How to Shop for a Top-Quality Portfolio

The Origins of My Investment Philosophy . . . The First C: Your Common Sense . . . The Second C: Your Comfort Zone . . . The First D: Diversification . . . The Second D: Discipline

Whom You Need and Why You Need Them . . . With So Many Choices, How Do You Decide? . . . Where Do You Begin? . . . Picking and Choosing . . . Scheduling Your First Working Appointment . . . Some Tips for Working Successfully with Your "A Team"

Separating Your Emotions from Your Money . . . Your Money Is a Reflection of Your Net Worth, Not Your Self-Worth . . . Controlling Your Money Instead of Letting It Control You: Choosing Your Investment Strategy . . . Risky Business . . . Market Strategies . . . What about Bonds? . . . Two Investment Strategies That Always Work . . . Be An Investor—Not a Trader . . . Market Timing versus Buy and Hold . . . Stop Loss . . . When the Shoes No Longer Fit . . . The Esther Berger Tried-and-True Chicken Approach to Investing . . . Tax Losses, Mutual Fund Switches, and the Wash Sale Rule . . . Knowing How to Take a Tax Loss

On October 18, 1991, Louis Rukeyser reported on his PBS television show "Wall Street Week" that a *Woman's Day* magazine survey of fifty thousand American women asked whether they would rather be rich, beautiful, famous, or younger. Fully 71 percent said they'd take the money and run!

Introduction . . .
Finances, Femininity, and Fear

Two years ago a client of mine received $300,000 as part of her divorce settlement. She immediately took to her bed for five days. Every day I called her and asked, "How are you doing, Patty?"

Every day her response was the same: "Esther, I can't cope with *this*. I'm going back to bed."

This was not the end of her fifteen-year marriage. *This* was the $300,000.

On the sixth day Patty called me and declared, "Esther, I'm giving the money back. I don't need it. I don't want it. And if I keep it, I'll just mess it up. That's it. It's settled. I'm giving it back." While I heard a great sigh of relief from her end of the line, I was fuming—another woman convinced she couldn't manage her money before she even tried! I wondered how many men would take to their beds after receiving the same lump sum.

But I understood Patty's anxiety about being responsible for so much cash, which even by Beverly Hills standards still counts as serious money. As a women's financial consultant, certified financial planner, and licensed stockbroker, I am familiar with the common fear so many women have about managing, handling, and investing their money. I suggested a reasonable solution that I thought would make Patty feel more comfortable.

"Patty, let's put your money in a tax-free money market account for a year and forget about it. Just pretend that it doesn't exist. Your money will be quietly and safely earning interest—and most important, your money will be doing something for you. After a year if you still don't want it, I'm sure your ex-husband will take it back."

I was dead serious about Patty giving the money back, but only after having enough time and emotional distance to make that decision. Reluctantly she agreed to my plan.

As she began to rebuild her life, Patty enrolled in a master's program in education and decided to teach preschool again. She had given up her teaching career shortly after she got married.

At the end of the year Patty was finally ready to accept the $300,000 but had no idea what to do with it. After a panicky phone call from her, I met with Patty and together we calmly planned her investments.

We first earmarked 20 percent of her $300,000 for living expenses. This included Patty's graduate school tuition and child-care costs for her two daughters, ages seven and twelve. We left another 10 percent in a tax-free money market account for emergency expenses and short-term cash needs. We also opened separate custodial accounts for her daughters' college education expenses. With the remaining balance of her lump-sum divorce settlement, still a healthy $180,000, we created a conservative investment portfolio of Treasury securities, tax-free municipal bonds, and blue-chip stocks that paid quarterly dividends. Patty could reinvest the income from these dividends or use them for additional living expenses.

It's been three years since Patty's divorce, and her feelings about handling her money have completely changed. Not only is she happy about the cash settlement she received, she's also very involved in choosing her investments. Patty realizes how important it is for her to be in control of the financial decisions that affect not only her future, but her daughters' futures as well.

You may find Patty's story hard to believe, even ridiculous. Getting used to having an extra $300,000 isn't what many of us think of as a hardship. But what can't be taken lightly is the fear Patty once had of handling her money.

This is not an exaggeration, and Patty's situation was not unique. I have found that regardless of age, income, or life-style, *the fear of "doing" money* is a common denominator among almost all women.

I remember watching one of the national morning talk shows that was airing a five-part series on women and money. During one segment their guest was a woman who at the time was a top executive for a leading entertainment company and was certainly a major financial decision maker at that company. Every day, at work, her opinions affected millions of dollars of corporate cash.

When the talk show host asked her how she felt about her ability to handle her own personal finances, I *wasn't* shocked when she stated bluntly:

"I fold. I can't do it."

She continued, "For example, when it came to deciding which mutual fund to pick in my pension plan, I didn't know one from the other, so I just checked the box that sounded best. It had the word *government* in it, so I figured it was safe."

What both of these women from opposite ends of the spectrum are saying is that their fear of handling, investing, and managing any amount of personal money is so overwhelming that it prevents them from taking charge of their financial lives. They have little or no sense of their "money selves": the ability to handle, manage, invest, and simply understand what money can do for them—especially how women can make their money grow.

Even the most take-charge women in the country have difficulty taking charge of their money. This point was brought home to me vividly in January 1991 when I had the privilege of speaking to the Senior Professional Women's Association at the Pentagon. My topic was "Women and Money." In all humility I must admit that I was probably the only non-Ph.D. in the room that afternoon.

I was amazed as these intelligent, competent, top-notch Washington women—many with backgrounds in statistical analysis—asked me the same questions that almost every other women's audience across the country has asked me: "What is a T-bill?" "How is it different from a CD?" "Are mutual funds good investments?" "What is a Ginnie Mae?"

Their questions were not complicated. Most of them stemmed from nothing more than not understanding the language of money, much less its nuances.

- What does owning a stock really mean?

- What's the difference between a stock and a bond?

- Are stocks always riskier than bonds?

- Why do stocks go up and down?

- What makes the stock market move so dramatically in one day?

These commonly asked questions and many others will be answered as you read this book. And the good news is that the answers will be in English, not in bankerspeak or brokerese.

Not understanding the language of money is one of the major stumbling blocks for any woman trying to make sense of her financial life. How can a woman expect to feel comfortable in the world of money, to participate actively in the world of money, if she doesn't understand or speak its language? This inability to communicate in a world from which a woman already feels alienated only adds to the existing fear and anxiety she has about her financial ability.

This is why, day after day, my office is filled with women who are very bright and competent yet at the same time are telling me that they can't get a grip on their financial lives. While these women confess that they don't even know where to begin, they all express the desire to develop their money selves.

And this is why after my column, "Why Women Fear Money," appeared in *Newsweek,* I received hundreds of letters and phone calls from a wide range of women across the country: "Esther, I feel as if your column were written to me personally. What do I need to do?"

Not only were there letters and calls from affluent women who already had investment portfolios reflecting the money they had earned themselves or acquired through divorce, widowhood, or inheritance, but I also heard from women who had a hard time just paying their monthly bills. Some had never worked outside their homes, while others held top-salaried positions and just couldn't manage to budget. Regardless of what any of these women did, or how much money they had or were making—their response to my column was the same: *They recognized their need to feel and be money smart.*

This need is increasing as our earning potential continues to grow and women come into additional money through widowhood and divorce.

More women are managing more money than ever before. Consider the following figures:

- Fully 35 percent of all estates in excess of $5 million are currently controlled by women.[1]

- More than 60 percent of all women work outside the home.[2]

- Women pay 56 percent of all family bills.[3]

- More than 5.4 million businesses in the United States are owned by women.[4]

- By the year 2000, 50 percent of all businesses in this country will be female-owned.[5]

Yet according to a 1991 Oppenheimer Management Corporation nationwide survey concerning women and their financial acumen:

- Only 9 percent of all women describe themselves as "very confident" when making an investment decision.

- Women between the ages of thirty-five and fifty-four are the least knowledgeable; 71 percent said that they did not know how to invest.

- Of this age group, 37 percent have never made an investment decision. An identical number said they spend no time on their savings and investments.

And surveys taken in 1992 revealed the following:

- While women are widely responsible for day-to-day management of household finances, only 12 percent make investment decisions on their own.

- Eighty-nine percent had no idea of the level of the Dow Jones Industrial Average.

- Sixty-two percent said that they didn't understand how a mutual fund works.

• Sixty-nine percent said they didn't know that stocks have historically outperformed bonds, CDs, savings accounts, and money market instruments.

• Fifty-two percent said they feel financially unprepared for retirement.

• Yet fully 82 percent of these women believe that they will be solely responsible for their own financial well-being at some point in their lives.

And they are absolutely right. According to the United States Bureau of the Census:

• Forty-eight percent of all women aged sixty-five and older will be widowed in their lifetime.

• Fifty percent of all women who married within the last twenty years will divorce.

• Ten percent will choose to remain single.

• At some point in their lives, an overwhelming majority of American women will have to bear responsibility for their own financial security.

As these statistics show, with so much financial responsibility inevitably becoming a part of every woman's life, women can no longer afford to be uncomfortable about managing their money. But because they still are, thousands of women lose hundreds of thousands of dollars a year due to poor advice, miscalculated investments, and, more often than not, simple neglect.

Putting your money in the bank and forgetting about it isn't good enough, because inflation and taxes consistently erode capital and purchasing power. Even at a low 4 percent annual inflation, money loses almost half its value in less than eighteen years. Therefore, those of you who avoid taking financial responsibility today will find that you have less money tomorrow. This means that by doing nothing, you are in fact doing something: losing money.

Managing our money or, at the very least, understanding where our money is and how our money is growing is a necessity and every woman's right—every woman's entitlement. This is not just another "women's issue" being tossed around. The bottom line is that a woman can no longer tolerate feeling financially uninformed because the quality of her life, especially her future, depends on her financial know-how. Ultimately, money determines our survival.

Just as the economy is in a state of constant change, so are our personal lives. Where is a woman's guarantee that someone—a male someone—will always be there to take care of her? Yet as little girls, isn't that exactly what so many women were taught? Believing this is what I call "the great illusion."

Supporting this illusion were television role models that, depending on our age, we either grew up with or watched while we did the housework: June Cleaver, Carol Brady, and Margaret Anderson of the wonderfully titled "Father Knows Best." These were women at home —perfectly coiffed and always smiling while their men were out conquering the business world. They lived a life of shirtwaist dresses and skinned knees as they played mistress to the perfect pot roast. "Honey, I'm home!" was their call to attention. They beamed as they greeted their precious breadwinner at the door.

No wonder most of the men in our lives, as well as our own mothers and fathers, just didn't get it when, collectively, women began to claim their place in the working world in the 1970s and even earlier. In fact, I'm not sure if we knew what we were getting into at first ourselves, trotting off to work in our navy blue suits and floppy bow ties—thinking we had to look and act like men because we were on their turf. When women entered the working world it went against *all* of our social conditioning.

But we hung in there and made steady, and sometimes incredible, inroads into the workplace as the men in our lives either adapted or, in some cases, left. Having dinner on the table at 6:00 P.M. was no longer a sure thing, and "daddies" had to learn how to carpool.

The days of women being taken care of are pretty much over—if indeed they ever really existed. The fact is that fathers die, marriages end, and lovers leave, voluntarily or by invitation. These endings, which can happen at any age, are a woman's reality. Not only do they cut close to the heart, they cut close to, if not through, the purse strings as well.

Given all of this, added to the fact that I work in the male-dominated world of finance—a world in which I'm still referred to by some of my male colleagues as "honey"—I realized that it was time for me to write a book that would make it possible for every woman to be money smart. It was time for me to share with every woman the money secrets I have learned that could give every woman control over her financial life.

But this meant that I would have to write something more than a terrific "how to do money" book—chock full of financial tips and investment strategies that I have found useful and successful.

Of equal importance would be a book that acknowledges the psychological gap that has existed between women and money for centuries, because before any woman can be money smart she must believe that it is possible. As long as any of us feels that we can't do something, we won't because we are not receptive to the information at hand. It's as though we've hung a "Do Not Disturb" sign on our brains.

You know, I've never had a man walk into my office and tell me he's financially inept. In fact, he usually assumes he knows a lot more than I do, and I wonder why he even wants my opinion.

Conversely, an incredibly bright woman will enter my office and before I can count to ten will start telling me how stupid she is. She might be running a successful home, career, or both—but still she'll tell me how embarrassed she feels about her inability to handle money. She'll even question whether or not handling her money is something she *should* be doing and whether she truly *can* do it.

When it comes to women and money, why this psychological gap? It has been created and perpetuated, generation after generation, by the belief that financial know-how involves a secret, mysterious knowledge intrinsic only to men—that there are, in fact, money secrets that men never tell women.

Historically, women have been programmed to think that money is male—that only men can deal the dollars. Consequently the majority of women weren't raised to feel comfortable with money, except spending it. Handling money wasn't their prerogative. It was some-thing they didn't need to know about.

And God help the woman who volunteered her opinion about financial decisions or even asked about how the money was being saved or invested. To do so wasn't feminine. It wasn't ladylike. In fact, women who prized their financial independence were told they would end up alone with only their money to keep them warm at night. Not a very positive message, was it?

All of these money myths and misperceptions, stemming from deeply ingrained, traditional attitudes, continue to feed women's fears about their ability to handle money. While most women realize these fears are out of sync with contemporary thinking, they're still afraid to take financial control. If they do, they believe that any mistakes they make will not only leave them appearing foolish or inept, but will lead to disaster. Many women envision themselves alone and penniless—they have "bag lady" nightmares.

Their conclusion?

Women and money don't mix.

Their solution? Put it in the bank: the yields may not keep pace with inflation—but at least it's safe! Or better yet, why not just hand the money over to a husband, brother, father, boyfriend, or business man-ager? That way they can pretend it doesn't exist and at the same time know that their money is where it belongs. In the hands of a man. After all, the world of finance is cloaked in mysterious secrets, creating a dollar fraternity to which only men are admitted.

These outdated attitudes, if not changed, are going to lead to seri-ous financial problems for women. While women fear making invest-ment mistakes, the real threat to their financial future is their lack of knowledge, their dependence on others to make financial decisions, and their inability to take action because of their fears—and because they just don't know where to begin.

The world is full of women like Patty, who have been left through death or divorce and suddenly have to manage their finances as well as everything else. Although the majority of women don't end up as well off as Patty, if they do, they are usually victims waiting to happen —either by losing their money to taxes and inflation or by allowing some unscrupulous person to lose it for them.

Whether we work outside the home or not, whether we are single or married, doesn't it make sense that taking charge of our money is the natural progression of where we have come from and where we are going; that it is a vital part of our evolution as women? It's a priority that needs to be addressed now, not when we suddenly have to deal with a life crisis, backed into a corner with few or no options.

I think that there is something fundamentally wrong that in the 1990s so many women still feel uninformed, childlike, and even stupid about money. We've come too far not to conquer this final frontier. We can't change the history of women and money, but we can determine the future of women and money—and we must!

So where to begin? If you are like most women, you are probably convinced that since you don't know the money secrets, at best it will take years of studying and reading before you will be equipped to enter the financial world. Wrong!

Perhaps the most important money secret of all, the one money secret more important than all the others combined, is that there is nothing mysterious about money. Investing isn't rocket science. Believe it or not, the "average woman" in Omaha may have as much chance of making money in the financial markets as any pro on Wall Street.

In this book you will find the necessary safe haven where you can confront your money fears as you realize that the world of finance is *not* cloaked in mysterious secrets known only to men. As your fears begin to diminish, you will find yourself more and more receptive to the valuable information provided; the valuable information you need to take control of your financial life.

You'll learn how to set goals and define your short-term and long-term investment objectives. You'll learn the up side and the down side of owning stocks, bonds, CDs, and real estate. And you'll learn how to make sound, smart investment decisions based on your common sense *and* your intuition.

Many of your investment decisions will be contingent on your age and personal life-style, whether you're single, married, or married with children. Your financial needs, interests, and priorities are different at every age and stage of life.

Certainly the financial concerns of a twenty-year-old are vastly different from those of a woman turning forty. Not only do they have different financial priorities, but their life expectations and experiences are not the same. A woman in her twenties often feels invincible as her whole life stretches before her. She may be vulnerable to financial pitfalls that someone in her forties or fifties is acutely aware of—probably because the older woman has already made some of these mistakes!

The fortysomething woman is beginning the second half of her life. Her children are leaving home. The workplace may beckon for the first time or, in some cases, after an extended "time out" for child rearing. Statistically, divorce is more likely now than at any other time. The fortysomething woman may have to cope with the emotional trauma that comes with this life change while she takes charge of her financial life for the very first time.

Things she may never have thought of—like retirement planning and life insurance—will involve serious decisions. But this is her opportunity to make wise financial decisions that will safeguard her money and secure her future.

Those of you who are sixtysomething or more may also be confronting your finances for the first time if you have been widowed. You may have inherited your husband's investment choices and, along with them, his investment advisers—none of whom you may like or trust. You may feel as inexperienced as a twentysomething woman just starting out, but it's not too late to make changes.

A final P.S. before you begin. Women are *not* money stupid. Many, however, are financially uneducated. Never forget that there is a world of difference between the two. Regardless of where you are in your life, the only two tools you need to feel and be money smart are an open mind and the willingness to learn.

Henry Kravis is a partner at the leveraged-buyout firm of Kohlberg Kravis Roberts & Co. He is widely regarded as one of the biggest "deal makers" on Wall Street. He also happens to be married to fashion designer and socialite Carolyne Roehm.

The name Henry Kravis may sound familiar. In 1989 his firm took RJR Nabisco private in the single largest deal that has ever been done in this country (or in any other country) to date.

In 1990 Henry Kravis was invited to speak to a gathering of the Financial Women's Association of New York. Eager to hear details of the RJR deal, the audience settled back to listen. Here is what they heard:

> I'm sorry my better half, Carolyne Roehm, couldn't be here today. She could speak to you about something you would probably be more interested in hearing about—fashion. (quoted in *Newsweek* magazine, March 19, 1990)

I am told that Kravis's audience greeted this statement with a resounding chorus of boos and hisses. As well they should have.

Kravis's implication was crystal clear: Sure you women invited me here to talk about the RJR deal, but wouldn't you rather, in your heart of hearts, in your soul of souls, talk about fashion?

If Henry Kravis could deliver this kind of message to the best and brightest financial professionals in America *who just happen to be female,* what is his message to other women across the country? To women in Cleveland, Ohio, and in Portland, Oregon, who are just starting to learn about money?

The presumption that women would rather talk about fashion than finance speaks to every stereotype surrounding the issues of finances, femininity, and fear. The implication is that "real" women—"ladies," if you will—are interested in fashion first, money maybe.

The more insidious message is that, even in the 1990s, women still have to choose between fashion and finance because they are mutually exclusive.

Apparently it's impossible to be both financially astute *and* fashionably attired, although men—including Henry Kravis—manage to do it all the time. But do women have to choose between being well dressed or being well heeled? I think not!

Nor do we have to choose between being successful and being happy. Or between having money in our lives or having men in our lives. They are *not* mutually exclusive. Not now, not ever.

PART ONE

Taking

Charge of

Your Money:

What's the

Bottom Line?

IF I'VE NEVER INVESTED BEFORE, HOW MUCH DO I NEED TO GET STARTED?

 "How much" is not nearly as important as "when." If you put off investing until you have "enough," you may never begin. The object is to start slowly, start small (if small is what you have), but *start*.

Secret #1 . . .
Men Aren't Born Money Smart: Defining Your Financial Goals

Contrary to popular belief, men do not exit the womb knowing everything there is to know about money. Men are not born money smart. In fact, their supposed expertise has been acquired and cultivated through repeated exposure over a long period of time. It has been handed down from father to son. And of course there is the obvious: for centuries, at every turn and at every level, men made the money. And those who made it owned it and controlled it. If women had been equal participants, they'd be money smart, too. This is why I always say, "Men aren't born smart—they just got a head start!"

A recent study by the National Education Association reported that girls and boys mirror one another in language arts and mathematics until twelve or thirteen years of age. Then there is a tremendous divergence. Suddenly girls seem to excel in language arts and boys in math and science. This has nothing to do with aptitude. It involves the social conditioning that comes with puberty.

Little girls are not raised to believe that they will be financially responsible for their families' futures—much less their own. Is it any wonder that they get the message loud and clear, even when it's subliminal, that it's okay if they don't understand math and science? It's not expected of them and they're "really" not supposed to understand. It's too male. Little girls have always been steered away from traditionally male things—especially money.

Society conditions us. Our parents condition us. And the coeducational school system reinforces this conditioning.

Research done by psychologists at educational institutions (including Harvard and the University of Southern California) indicates that coeducation fosters an environment in which boys dominate at the expense of girls. In one study teachers who viewed more than one hundred videotapes of coed classrooms were amazed at what they consistently saw:

• Boys are called on four times as often as girls.

• Boys are interrupted less frequently.

• Boys dominate discussions, are taken more seriously, are questioned more, and are challenged more to speculate and take risks.

• Boys also dominate science labs and computer rooms, while most girls avoid this "male" territory because they don't feel comfortable there. Most girls are convinced that they can't be as smart as boys in math and science.

This study also revealed that when girls are successful academically, they *still* feel that their success is at odds with their femininity. Regardless of their accomplishments, most girls expect to play supporting roles in their adult lives. They will become the nurturers. Conversely, the onus is on little boys to grow up to be financially responsible for their families. And even if theirs is a two-income family, often with their wives earning more than they do, men still expect to handle and manage the money.

As grown women, is it any wonder that we react like frightened children, full of self-doubt and fear, as we attempt to take charge of our financial lives? How can we feel differently when the knowledge we need has been kept from us for most of our lives?

Taking Responsibility

Until recently the complexion of money was so completely masculine (you don't think a woman invented the twin concepts of "bull" and "bear" market, do you?) that female interest was consistently discouraged, if not virtually disallowed. And it wasn't until 1972, because of one gutsy lady, that women were permitted to hold membership on any of the financial exchanges—or even permitted on the trading floor.

This take-charge lady was an active investor who traded through a major brokerage firm. Before leaving on a vacation, she requested that her broker buy five corn contracts at the Chicago Board of Trade.

When she returned she was delighted to find that the price of corn had gone way up. Eager to discuss her profits, she called her broker, who told her, "I'm sorry—our policy is that women are not allowed to trade commodities."

Not one to hesitate, this woman immediately sued the brokerage firm and won her case. Since then the doors to the financial world have been open to women—but most are still afraid to step in.

It would be foolish for any woman to presume that men will welcome her into the world of money, because it is the world of power. And nobody likes giving up power. No wonder most men feel threatened when women start taking control of their financial lives. But we can't expect men to change their negative attitudes about us handling money until we initiate the change within ourselves.

What affects change? When an ongoing situation just isn't okay anymore. Women have finally progressed to the point where they're more than uncomfortable with their lack of financial acumen—they're angry! Especially frustrated are those who are part of the work force. From these women I hear, "I'm out there making it, so there's no reason I can't be managing it, too! I'm entitled!"

Many women intuit this truth on a subconscious level, but their social conditioning and fear prevent them from realizing it on a conscious level, where they could take action. Others are very aware of their feelings, but they don't know how to express them or how to begin to change.

The twentysomething woman who is starting a career may be torn between a desire for financial independence and the hope that she'll find a male partner who will take control for her. While the financial barriers have been removed (at least in theory), the psychological barriers remain.

"Can you believe I've even put off buying a stereo?" says Megan, twenty-three, a bright, vivacious research assistant at a prominent advertising agency. "I just don't feel comfortable making decisions all by myself—especially decisions involving money. I don't even want to buy a stereo on my own, much less make investment decisions where I could really mess up." This from the mouth of a competent, otherwise confident twentysomething woman.

Without a doubt, those of us who are fortysomething are a generation of women in money transition. Although most of us haven't been encouraged to understand money in a big way, we also haven't exactly made the extra effort to learn. I know many women who run their own businesses, earning three to four times as much as their husbands —and yet still allow their husbands to manage their money even though deep down inside they know this is wrong.

And there are countless sixtysomething women who have never worked outside the home. Is there any doubt about who controls the family money? I remember hearing a story from one of my colleagues about the husband who gave his wife money to buy *herself* a new car. But there were conditions: the car had to be a Buick, and it had to be white. Obviously this man regarded the family money as his money. When it came to family finances, his wife had no latitude, no say-so. Unfortunately this put her in the same position as a little girl whose daddy gave her money and said, "But you have to spend it the way I tell you." When we women don't have jurisdiction over our financial lives, it's as though we're little girls all over again.

We've been co-conspirators in our lack of financial experience. Men have wanted to keep us as little girls, and we've cooperated because we've liked the idea of being taken care of. But it's time that we own up to our own issues and take responsibility for where we are right now. Too many of us still cop out, saying, "My husband handles it," rather than taking the time to understand the family finances.

Every time I give a speech the first question I ask is, "How many of you feel good about what you're doing professionally?" Lots of hands go up. Then I ask, "How many of you feel good about how you're handling your money, your family finances, your investments?" Hardly a hand goes up.

I ask them why they're not handling their money—why they don't feel good about it. Some of the common responses I get are (1) "I don't have time for it"; (2) "I'm not really interested in it"; (3) "Nobody has ever explained it to me"; (4) "I really don't know enough about it"; or (5) "I know I need to do this, *but* . . ."

Many women who come to me after a divorce complain that the reason they're financially uninformed is that their husbands never explained anything to them. What I always want to know is, *Did they ask?* And if they asked and their husbands were not cooperative, what kept them from finding out the answers on their own? There are plenty of books, seminars, and adult education courses on various aspects of finance. If women really want the information, it's out there.

We women have to take responsibility for where we've been, apply the *common sense* that tells us it's not wise for us to be there anymore, and *discipline* ourselves to move forward. Once we begin to develop our financial knowledge, we will be empowered by being in control. It feels good to flex your money muscles!

I have no doubt that we are all capable of achieving this. Why? Because I've worked with many frightened women who went from knowing nothing about money to taking total charge of their financial lives. Ultimately their desire, regardless of what motivated it, overpowered their fear.

Just *beginning* is the secret. In fact, beginning is everything—because once you get started, you'll realize that it's not that difficult to catch up with men. And as you learn more, you may notice that most of the men who talk money in a big way don't really know what they're talking about!

What's Wrong with This Picture?

Women are in the workplace, and women are controlling money. Yet they say they don't know how to invest, they don't know what a mutual fund is, and they have no idea how to compare the performance of one investment with another. Women may have discovered their earning power in the 1970s and 1980s, but they have yet to discover the power of investing. The power of money.

This isn't news to you.

You know it.

You get it.
And you don't like it!
Then what's the problem?

For starters, how about the financial professionals who ask to talk to your husband when they call—even if you're not married? There's no doubt that women are treated with less respect than men. It's still that same head-patting mentality that goes hand in hand with the unintelligible language. You know, the brokerese and bankerspeak. I'm convinced that these people perpetuate a mystery around money that doesn't really exist on purpose.

Why? Because they want to keep the power where it "belongs." With men. The twentieth-century version of the Golden Rule is, "Whoever has the gold, rules."

Ironically, a 1992 survey by *Money* magazine indicated that women make better financial decisions than men. *Money*'s survey of financial planners, stockbrokers, money managers, psychologists, and academics found five common characteristics associated with women that are also the hallmarks of smart financial decision making:

- Women ask questions

- Women seek help

- Women avoid risk

- Women do their homework

- Women set goals

While women tend to underestimate their knowledge, men tend to think they know it all. And they rarely ask for help. Ever notice that even when a man is obviously lost, he'll circle the same 7-Eleven store ten times before he'll stop and ask, "Which way?" A woman immediately pulls over and asks for help.

Why this difference? Because men have a preconceived notion that it's not masculine to ask for help. They have to be absolutely self-reliant. To ask for help makes them sound needy, helpless—*female!*

Again, it's about our social conditioning. Women have been raised to think that they can't—and are not supposed to—take care of themselves. Men, on the other hand, are supposed to take care of themselves *and* their women. They do *not* ask for help.

Women also set goals. Because they typically worry more about the future than men do, women are more likely to be savers than spenders. They plan.

Ironically, it is a woman's mentality that is going to succeed in the financial reality of the 1990s.

You see, wealth building will be much more difficult in the 1990s than it was in the 1980s and in previous decades.

Since 1980 rates on short-term investments have dropped 72 percent. This is happening at a time when most nondiscretionary expenses—including insurance, taxes, and health care—are on the rise. With interest rates expected to continue falling through the mid-1990s, it's going to be increasingly difficult to accumulate wealth—and even to keep pace with inflation.

Individual tax rates are likely to go up. Even a two-income family is going to have a tough time making ends meet. And providing a college education for your children isn't getting any cheaper.

During the recession in the early 1990s, a large number of people found themselves out of work and eventually had to settle for lower-paying jobs. Those who kept their jobs may have had to take a cut in pay.

If there was ever a time for women to step in and take charge of their money, it's now. Women have all the traits of excellent investors. And we have the *ability* to be excellent investors.

This is why women must confront, once and for all, any questions of financial entitlement and control. Taking financial responsibility is critical in terms of achieving security, prosperity, *and* maturity. What's at stake involves much more than dollars and cents.

The time for action is now. It's clear that at some point in their lives, nearly all women will have to take responsibility for their own financial well-being by virtue of widowhood, divorce, or opting to remain single. The more control a woman exercises over her finances on a day-to-day basis, the more capable she will be of making critical choices in the event of her spouse's death, a divorce, or other sudden life changes.

Defining Your Financial Goals

But how do you begin? By first defining, to the best of your ability, your financial goals. To help you get started, let me ask you one simple question I ask all of my new clients:

WHAT DO YOU WANT YOUR MONEY TO DO FOR YOU?

Whenever I ask this question, the answer I usually get is, "I want to make money!" This is a great sentiment—but it's the wrong answer.

You really need to quantify—it's not enough to say you want to make money. You have to decide specifically what your financial goals are and how much risk you're willing to take to attain them.

Keep in mind that your financial goals will change at different stages of your life. Deciding to marry, receiving an inheritance, or starting a family can alter your financial goals significantly. So can divorcing, becoming a widow, or losing your job.

If you are unclear about your goals, consider the following questions and write down your answers. This will give you a starting point and a sense of your position in the financial world at this time:

1. What is your income? Do you expect it to change within the next twelve months?

2. What is your accumulated debt? How much of it is credit card debt? How much interest are you paying to borrow?

3. Do you have a savings account? If so, where is it and how much is in it? What percentage interest are you earning on your money?

4. Do you have an investment portfolio? Did you make the investments or were they acquired through an inheritance or divorce?

5. Do you understand each investment that you own? If not, make a list of the investments that you don't understand.

6. Do these investments feel right to you? What would you like to change? Do you think the investments suit your current needs?

7. Do you have long-term goals that you need to plan for or have already started planning for, like your children's college education and your own retirement?

8. What about short-term goals: Are you planning on buying a new car next year or taking an extended vacation?

9. How realistic are your financial goals and expectations? What changes are you willing to make to attain your goals?

From your answers, you should have a pretty good sense of where you are financially and the areas that need immediate attention. For instance, you may be one of the many whose debt far exceeds their savings. Or you may be thirtysomething but haven't begun any serious retirement investing or planning.

And don't feel embarrassed if you've never invested or if you don't have much money to begin investing with at this time. There are systematic savings programs that can invest money in a savings account or mutual fund for you every month. You can actually begin with as little as $25 a month. Investigate the different "low budget" programs that may be available to get you started.

One of the biggest mistakes you can make is to put off investing and retirement planning because you assume that you'll eventually marry and "he'll" take care of it. Do you figure men do the same thing, assuming "she'll" take care of it? I think not!

Now that you've defined your goals—how you want your money to work for you—it's time to put it to work, to invest it. The following questions will help you define your investment parameters.

1. How much money do you have to invest at this time?

2. For how long can you afford to invest this money? Three months? Three years? Thirty years? It's important that you define your time frame.

3. How much risk can you afford to take and remain comfortable? What is your risk tolerance?

4. Do you understand the difference between a growth-oriented investment and an income-oriented investment?

5. Do you need income from your investments or is growth more important to you at this time?

6. Do you understand that income-producing investments can be safe but provide little to no protection against inflation?

7. Do you understand that growth-oriented investments are riskier but will help hedge inflation?

I've had several twentysomething clients who acknowledge the need for financial planning but put it off, explaining, "Why do all of this now when I expect to be married soon?"

Indirectly these women are telling me that once they're married they expect their husbands to take care of their finances. This attitude reeks of "little girl" financial dependency! Why not enter into marriage as an adult with your own investments, your own ideas, and your own sense of financial responsibility?

Of course, wedding bells don't ring for everyone (perhaps by choice), and suddenly you're fortysomething. Then "panic" sets in and you're emotionally and financially vulnerable because you haven't done the proper planning.

Most women who come to me at this stage of life are so afraid of their uncertain financial future that they become much too conservative. Often their money is just sitting in a low-interest savings account or a money market that barely keeps pace with inflation.

If this sounds familiar, remember that you probably have over twenty income-earning years ahead of you. You can still earn the additional money that you'll need for retirement if you start creating a diversified portfolio that includes some good growth investments. You'll have to be willing to take some risk to make up for lost time. And if you've been primarily a spender, you're going to have to become a saver and an investor. Take comfort in knowing that financial goals can be established *and* realized. It's never too late.

This is the approach men take. Why shouldn't it be the same for you?

$ Whether you are twentysomething or sixtysomething it's never too late to establish savings habits that will stay with you for the rest of your life. How much should you save? First, figure out what's comfortable for you and then stretch that amount by 10 percent.

Secret #2 . . .
Money Is Sexy, but Sexless:
Building Your Money House

Jack is handsome, forty-six, graying elegantly at the temples, and dressed impeccably in a black pin-striped suit. As he enters the restaurant to join a client for lunch, the maître d' nods approvingly and shows him to his table. As he glances at the menu, two young women, seated across the room, gaze longingly at him.

"Oh, what I'd give for a man like that!"

"He's pure class—you can tell he's worked hard to make it to the top."

"I bet he's a wonderful husband . . . a loving father."

Diane enters the same restaurant, hoping her accountant, Sam, will be on time. She chooses to sit at the bar and wait because Sam is always very fussy about where he sits. Diane is thirty-two with pretty, short blond hair. She wears a tailored silk suit, sleek black heels, a Rolex watch, and rather large diamond earrings. The same two women who were checking out Jack start in on Diane.

"I wonder who she's sleeping with!"

"Probably some old guy with lots of money."

"Who wouldn't look sexy if they had some rich guy footing the bill?"

What's wrong with this picture?

These two women are assuming that Jack is sexy because he's worked hard for his success. But Diane's sexiness is attributed to "some old guy with lots of money" who is keeping her in style.

The truth?

Jack was born into a very wealthy family and inherited his father's business. He has a Malibu condominium as well as an estate in Connecticut. Yes, he's married—but he spends more time with his mistress in Malibu than with his wife in Connecticut. Being able to afford this life-style makes Jack feel powerful and sexy.

Diane is an executive secretary for a law firm in Beverly Hills, earns $40,000 a year, lives in a rented bungalow in Burbank, and drives a Chrysler LeBaron. She's never been married and enjoys her independence. Yes, she's sexy. She's very sexy. But she's not a kept woman.

Where does she get the money that makes her look like a million? Except for a $10,000 inheritance, she earns it herself and budgets, saves, and invests it wisely. Diane is not afraid of money—in fact, she loves it. It empowers her.

Diane is one of the new enlightened women who realize that knowing how to acquire money and knowing what to do with it once you have it are attributes to be admired and respected. She knows that money is sexy, but it doesn't take a man to make it. Anyone can make money. Anyone can invest money. Because although money is sexy, it is sexless.

Unfortunately, many women like the two who were comparing Jack to Diane still believe that the world of finance is male territory. And if by chance a woman successfully becomes a part of it, she's probably not very feminine or sexy.

I remember one news reporter, Jill, who came to my home for an interview. From the moment she entered my home I could tell she was shocked that I had a life outside my office. And when I introduced her to my husband and three sons, her mouth literally dropped open. It took her several minutes to get her bearings before she could begin the interview.

Later Jill confided, "I pictured you differently, Esther. Given what you do and the amount of money you manage, I figured you'd be a really aggressive, hard-driving businesswoman who would have no time to be a wife and mother. And no way could you be feminine or sexy."

When I say that money is sexy, my point is that when *you* handle, when *you* manage, when *you* invest, and when *you* deal with your money, it makes you sexy. But money in and of itself is sexless because it doesn't care who makes it. It has no hidden agendas. Money is an equal opportunity employer that's genderless. If you have any doubts about this, take note of its color. Money is green, not blue or pink. Or, more to the point—$100,000 earned by a man isn't worth any more than $100,000 earned by a woman.

I know that the majority of you were not raised to think about the money you would be capable of earning someday and how good you would feel taking charge of it. This would mean wheeling and dealing and making those big investment decisions just like a man. But the time has come for you to accept that it's very sexy to be in control of your money and that it doesn't undermine your femininity—it enhances it. Tell me what's attractive, sexy, or appealing about a woman who lives from hand to mouth or a woman who's frantic about her finances, and we'll have a different conversation.

So tune out the past. Change the channel. Erase the old tapes. Dispel any money myths that are self-limiting, and recognize that money is the great equalizer. In fact, financial know-how, in its own right, is just as sexy as a well-toned body—and considerably longer lasting!

Let's Get Physical! Physically Organized, That Is

In the last chapter you defined your financial goals. By doing this, you confronted your financial situation as it is, and you have some ideas about changes that need to be made. Now that you're mentally focused on your money, your next step is to buy yourself a "money house."

Your money house is where you will store anything and everything that pertains to your financial life. I recommend using a two-drawer filing cabinet. Your filing system doesn't have to be complicated. For starters, create separate files for

- bank statements and account information

- brokerage statements and investment records

- tax information

- retirement information

- insurance policies

- personal papers (like a birth certificate, passport, and so forth)

- bills

- credit card statements and receipts

- all other receipts

- warranties on any household appliances

Once you've created your money house, use it. This means emptying out all those shoeboxes full of the stuff you hate to deal with—your bills, receipts, tax information, and the like. Once you're comfortable in your money house, you will want to create subfiles. The point is to keep all of your financial data, information, and records together and organized so you'll always know exactly where everything is. You'll be amazed at the amount of time you'll save when you're paying bills, coping with income taxes, or getting the microwave you bought last month fixed without a hassle because you know exactly where the warranty is.

Know Where Your Money Is Going

Since you have a sense of your financial goals and you know in what areas you need to plan, go a step farther and take your financial inventory. This means sitting down with the past six months of your checkbook entries and receipts, including credit card statements. (If you haven't been keeping receipts, promise yourself that from now on you will.) Log in your income versus your expenses. You'll see exactly where your money is going.

Also make a separate list of purchases or expenses that weren't really necessary. By doing this you are pinpointing items that are eating up money that could go toward your savings.

This initial inventory will take you about two hours. It may seem like a horrible task, but once it's done you'll feel more at ease and definitely more in control, because you'll know exactly where you are financially. You'll also learn a lot about your spending habits. After this first inventory, a once-a-month assessment should take you no more than thirty minutes.

If you find that you're carrying debt on credit cards that charge between 18 and 21 percent interest, and at the same time you are earning much less than that on the money sitting in your bank account, pay off your credit card debt immediately. You'll still come out ahead even if you have to pay for checking until you bring your bank balance back to the minimum.

You Are Your Most Important Creditor

I don't care if you are twentysomething or sixtysomething—it's never too late to establish savings habits that will stay with you for the rest of your life.

The trick is to think of yourself as your most important creditor. This means that you get paid first. How much? I tell most women to first figure out what's comfortable for them and then to stretch that amount by 10 percent. You'll pay this amount to yourself by setting up a separate account that is not commingled with any of your other funds. It can be in the form of a savings account or a money market to begin with.

If you work on a commission basis and don't have a fixed monthly salary, figure out a reasonable percentage that you can take off the top of every commission check you get. Again, the idea is always to pay yourself first.

You can also establish your savings plan with a credit union. Employers can take money out of your paycheck and put it in the credit union. Some offer higher interest rates than your savings accounts or money markets. And find out whether or not your company has a payroll deduction program that can establish investments for you. This can be an automatic plan where "X" amount of dollars are taken out of every paycheck and are sent directly to your brokerage account or mutual fund company.

Some Common Savings Mistakes

Don't ever make the mistake of thinking, I'll save what's left after I pay my bills and cover my expenses, because nobody ever has anything left. This is why I always stress that you make yourself your number one creditor—first in line to be paid.

By doing this, you're always prepared for an emergency. Unfortunately life is full of them, and they usually involve cash in one way or another. Although ideally you should have a separate emergency fund, your savings can fulfill the need if necessary.

Again, if you are a free-lance or commission-based worker, you'll probably find it harder to save because you don't get paid on a regular basis. This is why you must take a percentage from every check you receive for your savings. Don't count on the "I'm sure it will come through" money you're supposed to receive as your savings. Because more often than not, for some reason or another, this money never materializes. Counting on "I'm sure" money can be financially fatal.

My client Anne was a newly successful songwriter when her divorce hit and wiped her out financially. She had no savings and knew that in September she and her two little girls would have to move because their rent was too high and her lease was up. Fortunately her agent had told her earlier in the year that she would be receiving a $20,000 royalty check sometime in July. Anne considered this "I'm sure" money her savings, and borrowed money from her friends, promising to pay them back the moment she received her check.

July came and went. Then August. On the last day of August Anne found out that there had been an error and that there would be no $20,000.

Now this was a woman in a pickle. She was recovering from a bad divorce, the "I'm sure" money had vanished into thin air, and she was up to her ears in debt to her friends. When her sixty-seven-year-old landlord offered her a free month's rent if she'd be "nice" to him, she didn't know whether to laugh or cry. Instead, desperate and frantic, Anne went to her parents for a loan. Fortunately they had the money to help her out.

Horrified, humiliated, and humbled, Anne learned one of the biggest lessons of her life: the importance of having a *real* savings plan —and making saving a regular habit.

Beating the Credit Card Crunch
While Establishing Excellent Credit

After stressing the importance of saving, I'm now going to urge you to get a credit card if you don't have one. Why? To help you establish your credit rating.

Using your credit card, make small purchases that you know you can pay for as soon as you get the bill. Do this periodically, always paying the bill in full each month, and you'll have an excellent credit rating.

The down side of having a credit card is not being able to pay it off and consequently paying ridiculously high interest on your debt until you can. Should you find yourself becoming a credit card junkie, park your plastic somewhere safe until you've regained your self-control.

The beauty of properly used credit cards is the "float." You get up to twenty-eight days to use the credit card company's money. This means that you can earn up to twenty-eight extra days of interest on your money while it's still in your interest-bearing checking account. But remember: you've got to pay your credit card off in full each month. If you don't, the 18 to 21 percent you have to pay in interest can add up to a nightmare—and a nondeductible one at that!

When my husband and I bought a treadmill, the store offered us ninety days of free credit. This was terrific—except that they kept calling me, suggesting that I buy more and charge more as they continued to raise my credit limit. Good try, no sale.

At the end of the ninety days I paid off the treadmill in full, so I wasn't charged one penny of interest. This meant that for ninety days their money was in my checking account earning me interest. It didn't cost me a penny to borrow, and meanwhile I collected interest on the money I would eventually pay them. It makes me laugh to think that I made money while using my treadmill—I lost weight and gained interest!

Dealing with Your College Debt

Pay down your college debt before you hit thirty. Many of you may have gone through law school or medical school and have substantial education debts to pay off.

It's easy to forget about the money you borrowed once you are out of college because there are so many changes in your life. Chances are good that you'll be relocating to a new city. It may be several months to several years before the debt catches up with you—this means lots of back interest to pay, and it could also hurt your credit rating.

Buy Renter's or Homeowner's Insurance, but Don't Stop There

Besides having renter's or homeowner's insurance, I strongly encourage you to make sure you have adequate health and disability coverage. Evaluate your insurance needs realistically and resist the temptation to save money by being underinsured. Investigate the possibility of group coverage through your employer, although you should check to see if you can do better on your own through a personal insurance agent.

Family Planning

Once you start your family, you should start setting aside college education funds immediately. There are different ways to do this. Seek out information about custodial accounts and trust arrangements as soon as possible.

Why the big rush to start saving? Because college costs are astronomical—and climbing! According to the College Board, a nonprofit educational organization, the average costs for public and private colleges in 1991–1992 were $7,584 and $16,292, respectively. With costs increasing at 6 to 7 percent per year, by 2009 four years at a public college could cost $70,000, and nearly $200,000 at a private school like Princeton or Yale.

To have enough money, you'll need to save somewhere between $160 and $350 per month beginning the day your baby is born. (This assumes an 8 percent average rate of return and varies depending on the school you choose.)

If saving for college at this time seems impossible, given all the additional expenses new babies bring, you can begin with Series EE bonds, which are offered at denominations as low as $25.

Zero-coupon bonds are also good starting points for funding future college expenses because they can be bought in maturities timed to coincide with your child's freshman year and beyond. You don't collect any interest until you cash them in. What better way to enforce your savings? As you add to your college fund, be sure to hedge your portfolio with top-quality stocks for growth and inflation protection. (More information on zero-coupon bonds is offered on page 103.)

How the Value of Your Money
Can Go Up and Down at the Same Time

Is it possible to be losing money even when your investments are making money? Yes, if they are not keeping pace with inflation. Even though your dollars may be growing, they may not be growing fast enough. It may seem like you're winning the race, but you may be just running in place or, worse, being left behind.

INFLATION

Inflation basically means that it costs more dollars to buy the same goods and services today than it did yesterday. And it will cost even more tomorrow. If you read or hear on the news that "inflation is currently 4 percent," it means that your money will buy 4 percent less this year than it did last year. This means a real shrinkage of your real dollars. For example, if you spent fifty dollars on a birthday present for your mother last year, you're going to have to spend more to buy the exact same gift for your aunt Zelda this year.

Let me share an example of what inflation means to me:

My husband and I took a two-day vacation in early 1991 with our three sons. We had last been to San Diego five years before and had stayed in the same hotel and eaten at the same restaurants. We visited the same tourist attractions and took the same boat ride around Mission Bay. What was different this time around? Nothing—except the prices. Five years ago our vacation cost us $300. In 1991 the exact same vacation cost us $640—more than double! Now *this* is inflation, and it hurts! Unfortunately it doesn't go away, either.

Sometimes we hear very abstract terms on the nightly news about inflation. This is not terribly real to most of us. But it gets very real very quickly when it costs us twice as much today as it did five years ago to take our kids on vacation.

My Ten Commandments for Becoming Financially Independent

To support you as you create a sound, well-thought-out financial plan, here are my Ten Commandments for becoming financially independent. Copy these or photocopy them from the book and place them where you'll see them frequently. Whenever you begin to doubt your ability to make financial decisions, read them and forge ahead. Remember, your opinions and decisions are as valid as anyone else's.

1. Know that you're entitled to take charge of your finances.

2. Do not confuse lack of familiarity with lack of brainpower.

3. Ask questions until you understand the answers.

4. Make investment choices without fear of failure. Believe that you will succeed.

5. Trust your gut feeling. Go with your instinct.

6. Consider what's financially best for you—not just what's best for your loved ones.

7. Do not feel you have to excuse, explain, or justify your financial decisions.

8. Stop apologizing for investment mistakes. Everyone who invests makes mistakes.

9. Rely on *you* to take care of *you*. Believe in yourself.

10. Do not worry about what you haven't done. Focus on what you can do today.

Regardless of where you are in your life, know that you can begin financial planning now. Although you can never start too early, it's never too late to begin. When it comes to financial planning, the only mistake you can make is to put off doing it.

If you have children, educate them now. Think about it. What do you wish for your daughter or the daughter you may have someday? Isn't it to have a happy life and financial independence, never to "want" for anything? If marriage and children happen to be part of it, great! But isn't it most important to know that she can take care of herself?

I've taught my sons the value of saving, budgeting, and investing because once they grow up, they'll be on their own. My message to them is "I love you, and the greatest gift of love I can give you is self-reliance." And if I had daughters instead of sons, my message would be exactly the same, especially given what I've watched women go through as they try to overcome the money fears that keep them financially disenfranchised.

My friends who have daughters do not always give them this message, however. My best friend, Ava, has three daughters who are the same ages as my three sons. One of her daughters, Jerri, wants to be an attorney. I say good for her. And I tell my friend Ava that I'd like to talk to Jerri about which areas of the law are most lucrative.

Ava turns to me and says, "Esther, this is not about making money . . . this is about being happy."

To which I respond, "Ava, get a grip. This is about making money *and* being happy. They're not mutually exclusive."

It's time for women to wake up and smell the coffee!

$ Even at 4 percent annual inflation, money loses almost half its value in less than eighteen years. Therefore, the women who avoid taking financial responsibility today will find they have less money tomorrow. By doing nothing, they are, in fact, doing something: losing money.

Secret #3...
Don't Put Off Until Tomorrow: Planning for the Future

How many of you actually believe you're close to thirty, forty, fifty, or sixty years old? Personally, if someone asks me how old I am and I don't stop to think, I automatically say thirty-two—and here I am closer to forty than thirty! Although I've got years ahead of me before retirement, it seems like only yesterday that my sixteen-year-old was smiling in his crib.

We always feel that we have so much time, when in fact time goes by so quickly. Think about it. Do you believe how fast the last five years have gone by? What about the last ten?

Where were you ten years ago? Were you investing? Think about how much your investments might have grown by now if you'd started then.

I know that financial planning isn't on anyone's list of top ten fun things to do. But it's not as bad as cleaning out closets, either.

Forget about the mistakes of the past, about what you have or haven't done, and know that it's never too late to take control of your financial life—or too early! Whether you are twenty, thirty, forty, fifty, sixty, or then some, don't put off until tomorrow what you can and should start today—your financial planning.

Financial planning isn't just about investing. In fact, investing is only one component of financial planning. What financial planning really entails is putting your financial house in order. This means establishing credit, having a *growing savings,* planning for retirement and your children's college education, having appropriate insurance coverage, creating a will or trust, and monitoring your investments periodically to make sure they are still right for you. Financial planning is about understanding every aspect of your financial life—knowing what you've got, where you've got it, and where it should be going in the future. In addition, you should balance the investments you do make.

In working with women clients of all ages, I have found that each generation has specific financial planning needs due to different life expectations and experiences. And the mind-set of their generation greatly influences how they approach financial planning.

What follows is a generational profile and a general overview of basic financial planning for the twentysomething woman, the fortysomething woman, and the sixtysomething woman. Because investment planning should be individualized, based on risk tolerance and life-style—not just age—specific planning strategies will be covered in greater detail throughout the rest of the book. (The terms used may be unfamiliar, but they'll be discussed in depth in part 2.) Ideally, this initial overview will give you some sense of what you should have done or should be doing now and what you'll need to prepare for in the future.

You need to structure your portfolio as a money triangle. To stay within your comfort level, create the base or bottom third of your triangle with what I call "sleep at night investments." These investments are the safest of all. They will not make you rich, but they are stable and can provide you with income. These investments allow you to sleep at night because their value almost never changes.

The middle of your triangle is created by your "inflation fighters" —your growth investments, which increase in value and therefore counteract inflation—and should be extremely well diversified.

Finally, at the top of your triangle—if you can afford it and have the stomach for it—are your most aggressive growth investments. This is where you invest only as much money as you can afford to lose. For some clients, especially when it comes to retirement money, this top little triangle remains totally blank.

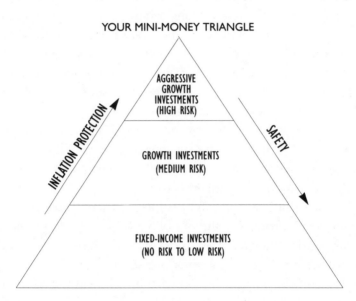

YOUR MINI-MONEY TRIANGLE

AGGRESSIVE
GROWTH
INVESTMENTS
(HIGH RISK)

INFLATION PROTECTION

SAFETY

GROWTH INVESTMENTS
(MEDIUM RISK)

FIXED-INCOME INVESTMENTS
(NO RISK TO LOW RISK)

The Twentysomething Woman: Twenty to Forty Years Old

At twentysomething you feel as if you've got the world on a string and that you can accomplish just about anything. You're invincible—you feel as if you'll live forever! You've got unlimited energy and are probably at your best physically. It's as though your life is a blank canvas—and it's up to you to paint the picture.

Your priorities at this time are pursuing your social life, completing your education, and establishing your career, not necessarily in that order.

Even though this is the 1990s, many young women still envision the man of their dreams riding up on that mythical white horse and whisking them away. Most of you have been raised to believe that regardless of how successful you become, ultimately a man will come into your life and take care of everything—including the money.

The truth of the matter is that if you marry at this time, your husband is probably no more prepared to handle the finances than you are. In fact, you are actually on even footing—but you don't realize it.

You may have been raised to believe that in a marriage men manage the money.

Most of you who start making money in your twenties have no idea what you should do with it. You tend to think short term because life seems eternal. Even though your thirties may bring a mortgage and babies, the money you earn in your twenties typically goes for rent, entertainment, beautiful clothes, and fun trips. Whatever is left at the end of each month just seems to slip through your fingers.

"I have definitely overextended myself and am now, quite literally, paying for it," explains Ellen, twenty-six, assistant to an East Coast literary agent. "Even now that I've stopped spending above my means, I still have to face the fact that I'm nearly four thousand dollars in debt."

Ellen, an independent, responsible young woman earning $26,000 per year, has paid her own bills ever since graduating from college and moving into her own apartment. "The trouble started when I got credit cards at Bergdorf Goodman and Bloomingdale's," she says, "plus an American Express card, MasterCard and a Visa. I was in credit card heaven, which I now know is credit hell."

Paying only the monthly minimum on her credit cards while she continued to overspend lulled Ellen into a false sense of financial security. Because she hated to balance her checkbook, she was never really sure how much money she had. When her bank started bouncing her checks for insufficient funds, reality hit Ellen. Hard.

"I finally had to borrow money from my father to pay off my credit cards. Imagine how that made me feel—like I was nine years old asking for another advance on my allowance," says an embarrassed Ellen.

Ironically, Ellen's older sister, Sasha, twenty-nine, had gone through a similar financial fiasco on a much larger scale only a year earlier. Sasha's financial situation became so severe that she was forced to declare personal bankruptcy.

"Sasha's experience followed by my own near disaster convinced me to get my financial act together," says Ellen. "I've cut up all my credit cards, am working overtime whenever possible, and I'm paying my father back every month like clockwork. I learned my lesson the hard way, and I hope I never, ever, have to learn it again!"

Following is your financial focus from twenty to forty, whether married or single:

$ Establish good credit and maintain it by avoiding credit card debt.

$ Begin a savings program the moment you get your first paycheck.

$ Establish an emergency fund. This is separate from your savings.

$ Start investing, either with the help of a financial adviser or through your company. The greatest percentage of your investments should be in growth-oriented investments be-cause you have so many inflation-fighting years ahead of you.

$ Buy health, life, and disability insurance and make sure you have adequate coverage.

$ Establish college funds for your children as soon as they are born.

$ Prepare for your retirement now. Investigate, research, and ask questions about the best plan for you to start put-ting your money into now.

The Twentysomething Generic Investment Plan: Growth stocks, especially recession-resistant companies with steadily increasing earnings; AAA-rated bonds; mutual funds. *Your emphasis is on establishing a retirement plan and building a growth portfolio.*

Most twentysomething women earning money for the first time enjoy spending it, not saving it. You assume that you'll just earn more money as you get older and the future will take care of itself.

It seems unnatural to start planning for retirement. In fact, it's in-conceivable to start any type of long-term financial planning. With so many prosperous years ahead of you, your attitude is "Why should I start now?"

Ironically, this is the most opportune time to start planning your financial future. It's much easier now than later to change any preconceived notions you have about your ability to manage money. The right money habits established now, including your spending and saving habits, will serve you in good stead for the rest of your life. This is why when you're twentysomething, financial planning should be your top priority—not something at the bottom of your "to do" list.

The Fortysomething Woman: Forty to Sixty Years Old

At fortysomething reality sets in as you begin to realize you won't stay young forever. In fact, in retrospect, your youth seems to have flown by. Whereas in your twenties and thirties you felt that *you* made life happen, in your forties and fifties life seems to be happening to you.

Your children leave home, your marriage may be going through transition, health problems pop up, and suddenly you may find yourself responsible for your elderly parents' care and well-being.

Unless you've remained single, you have gone from being a daughter to being a wife and mother. Now you may be wondering who you are and what your role in life is. Midlife crisis is real, and it can be frightening, because with the confusion comes the realization that only *you* are responsible for your life.

If divorce is a part of your fortysomething years, managing money may be a first-time experience for you. And even if you have been very hands-on with the family finances over the years, you may have to learn how to live on a lot less.

Conversely, you may have never even balanced a checkbook when suddenly a judge grants you a large divorce settlement. You kick yourself for being so money "stupid" all those years, and, terrified of financial responsibility and failure, you take to your bed. Or worse, you hand your money over to someone else to manage, hoping, if nothing else, that this will bring you peace of mind because you'll have less to deal with.

Following is your financial focus from forty to sixty, whether married or single:

$ Play financial catch-up, if necessary. Look at and understand all of your investment accounts. Consolidate, but don't keep all of your money in one place. Have at least one bank and one brokerage account.

$ It's never too late to start saving. If you are just starting, put away as much as you can to make up for lost time.

$ Make ongoing contributions to retirement plans. Two things will come into play: how much you can afford to put away on a regular basis and contribution limits. The annual maximum you can contribute in most retirement plans is $30,000. If you can save more, consider supplementing your retirement plan with a tax-deferred annuity.

$ Evaluate your investments. Look at the money triangle and make the necessary changes so that your percentage of growth investments is approximately equal to your age. For instance, if you are fifty, you'll want to have half growth and half income investments. If you're investing for the first time, use the money triangle to help you make disciplined investment choices.

$ Know your tax bracket. If you're in a high bracket, consider shifting some of your income-producing investments to insured tax-free municipal bonds.

$ If you don't own your own home, think about investing in real estate as an inflation hedge. Not only does it appreciate over time, but it provides you with a tax deduction on interest and property tax payments, as well.

$ Reexamine your health, life, and disability insurance to make sure you have sufficient coverage.

$ Make a will or establish a trust. If your gross estate is valued at less than $600,000, a will may be adequate. If it's more, think about establishing a trust. Talk to an attorney who specializes in estate planning before deciding.

> ***The Fortysomething Generic Investment Plan:*** In-
> sured tax-free municipal bonds; growth stocks; life insur-
> ance; tax-deferred annuity; real estate. *Your emphasis is on
> wealth building and increasing the value of your retire-
> ment portfolio.*

And if you're fortysomething, career-focused and financially successful, you're still afraid. You haven't managed your money very well,
although you may feel like a champion spender. You don't understand
your company's retirement plan, and you've never taken the time to
start investing—except for the IRA you've been contributing to every
year because your accountant told you to.

You realize that you may never marry (perhaps by choice), which
means you'll have only *you* to take care of *you* as you grow older.
That's when the panic sets in big time!

"I woke up in a cold sweat at three o'clock in the morning on my
fortieth birthday, convinced I was having a heart attack," recalls my
client Polina a week later. "I couldn't breathe and my heart was
pounding. I've never been so scared in my life."

Fortunately, Polina's "heart attack" turned out to be a major league
anxiety attack. "I was absolutely terrified," she says. "I was having the
worst 'bag lady' nightmare of my life, and it wouldn't go away even
after I was fully awake."

Polina, public relations director of a California-based corporation,
had just turned down her third marriage proposal. Happily single all
of her adult life, she had always managed both her career and her
social life exceptionally well. But not her money.

"I had saved nothing, spent everything, and had always assumed
that someone would get it all straightened out eventually," says Polina.
"I think the anxiety attack happened when I finally realized that the
'someone' was me and 'eventually' was now."

Single, divorced, or married, the life passages of fortysomething
women may be different but equally difficult. From a financial point
of view, though, they are definitely manageable. Even if you have to

make up for lost time or past mistakes, the good news is, it's very doable.

It's time to stop worrying about what you haven't done and take charge of your financial future. Today. Right now.

Although you may not have the benefit of eternal youth on your side, you do have the benefit of fortysomething years of life experience. From this you have developed a good internal barometer, a good sense of what does and doesn't work for you. Your instincts will more than compensate for any lack of financial know-how. I encourage women in this age group to trust their instincts when making financial decisions. Also talk to your financial professionals and ask questions until you understand.

The Sixtysomething Woman: Sixty Plus Years

As a sixtysomething woman you are at what I call the "revisiting" stage of your financial life. This means you should be reevaluating your insurance needs, your estate plan, and your investments. Ideally, your financial house should already be in order as you prepare for major life changes. These changes may include retirement (yours or your husband's), an increased need for health care, and, realistically, widowhood.

If you're married, statistics show that you have a 75 percent chance of outliving your husband. This is why my main concern for sixtysomething women is that they be financially secure before any of these life changes or crises occur. I don't mean to sound morbid, but there is so much emotional chaos following the death of a spouse, the last thing you want to have to think about is your money. Going from being a wife to being a widow is bad enough without having financial worries as well.

The best thing you can do for yourself at this stage of your life is to get very hands on about your money, especially if your husband has been managing the finances and making investment choices independent of you throughout your married life. The worst possible scenario is for your husband to pass away without your having a good understanding of your financial picture. You may not even know the financial advisers your husband has been working with, and when you meet them, you may discover they're not right for you.

I have a client, Bernice, whose husband, Walter, always dealt with a particular broker. After Walter's death the broker made Bernice feel that without him she would be lost financially. Because of her grief, she was vulnerable to his control. He refused to give Bernice a straight answer about anything, and she didn't dare antagonize him because she felt that he was the only living link she had to "Walter's money."

One day, several months after Walter's death, Bernice came to her senses and demanded to know how this broker was handling her portfolio. What stocks did she own? What kinds of bonds? Once again he tried to put her off, at which point she demanded a list of her investments and started making calls to other brokerage firms. Eventually she ended up in my office.

Bernice's story is an excellent example of how the sixtysomething woman can be a victim waiting to happen. People assume that just because you are sixtysomething, you are feeble-minded, when in fact you're totally competent. But if you're not prepared to take over your financial life, it's easy to be overwhelmed and to start believing that perhaps you really are incompetent and helpless when it comes to managing your money. This can make you an easy target for the many unscrupulous people who unfortunately do exist.

I think that the most loving, thoughtful thing a husband can do for his wife is help her understand their finances and prepare her to take over this part of her life should he die before she does. This includes introducing her to the financial advisers he's been using and letting her know that it's okay to look elsewhere if she feels uncomfortable with them. Often the sixtysomething woman is resistant to becoming involved financially because she doesn't want to deal with the two-fold impending reality of the loss of her husband and the sudden necessity of managing her financial life.

If you're a sixtysomething woman who has always been financially involved, don't start doubting your abilities now just because you're getting older. You may not be able to control the aging process, but you can still control your money.

I had one client, Sarah, who as a result of a severe stroke in her seventies moved to a nursing home because she needed constant care.

Following is your financial focus from sixty years on:

$ Review and understand your retirement plan because retirement is just around the corner.

$ Contact Social Security for an estimate of the benefits you can expect.

$ Shift some of your growth investments into income-producing investments. You may need this additional income to supplement your Social Security and pension benefits.

$ Know where all of your documents and important papers are located.

$ If your husband manages all the finances, ask him to make a list of your bank accounts, brokerage accounts, and other financial assets. Also, ask him for the names and telephone numbers of the financial advisers with whom he works.

$ Consider making lifetime gifts to your heirs to reduce the size of your estate. You can gift up to $10,000 per person per year *tax free* to as many people as you wish. If you are married, the maximum increases to $20,000. Besides reducing the size of your taxable estate, you'll have the pleasure of seeing your loved ones enjoy your money while you are still alive.

$ Make decisions concerning future financial and health care needs. Decide in advance who will make medical and financial choices for you should you become physically or mentally incapacitated, and execute the appropriate documents.

$ Review your will or trust and see if it needs revision. Things may have changed substantially since it was first drafted. Make sure its provisions reflect your current wishes.

The Sixtysomething Generic Investment Plan: Shift a portion of your portfolio to income-producing investments including tax-free municipal bonds, Treasury securities, and

> high-yielding common stocks. But don't move totally out of growth investments. *Your emphasis is on income and preservation of principal, but you still need to be concerned about inflation.*

But she still called the shots when it came to her investments. Although it was difficult for her to speak, she was determined that as long as her mind was unimpaired, she would control her money. Unfortunately, her physical deterioration continued. And when she sensed that the end was near, she had the presence of mind to delegate all the financial decision making to a relative whom she loved and trusted.

Of course, many sixtysomething women can expect to live well into their eighties and beyond. My grandmother Cecilia lived to be eighty-six and was as sharp as a tack till the day she died.

Most cultures around the world venerate age out of respect for the value of wisdom and experience. But in the United States, older people are considered either Cabbage Patch cute or helplessly fragile. They're not given credit for being the capable human beings that they are. And when you have enough people telling you that you can't manage your affairs, you start doubting your own ability. But remember that just being sixtysomething doesn't mean that you can't continue to make investment decisions—or even grab hold of the reins for the first time!

Thinking About Tomorrow Today

I have stressed the importance of retirement planning for the twentysomething, fortysomething, and sixtysomething woman. For good reason. Regardless of your age, *nothing* is more important than planning for your retirement. It should always be your first and foremost financial priority.

Unfortunately, though, most people think otherwise. According to

a July 1992 study conducted by the Gallup Organization, only 5 percent of Americans said they were concerned about retirement. Most
people ignore retirement planning, focusing instead on short-term
money issues like paying bills and worrying about job security.

Even among those aged fifty-five and older, retirement planning
ranked low as a major concern, with only 9 percent even mentioning
it. Meeting daily living expenses and health care took top priority.

And, of course, we all know people who say they're just too busy
enjoying life to worry about retirement.

A few years ago I had the pleasure of doing some investing for
Rosemary, a very wealthy and active eightysomething woman. When I
asked her when she planned to retire, she answered, "I've scheduled
my one hundredth birthday party at Disneyland . . . after that I'll consider retirement!"

What a classic comment about putting off retirement planning! Although many of us do this, few of us can afford the luxury that this
woman has. She's lucky—she's a very wealthy woman.

Retirement planning is misunderstood by most people. The common misperception is, "I don't have to think about it right now—it's
too soon!" Well, unless you're Rosemary's favorite relative and first in
line to receive an inheritance from her, it's never too soon to begin—
even if you're only twentysomething.

I've had a tough time convincing my sister-in-law Claire, twenty-
five, to start thinking about retirement planning. An apprentice architect only two years out of graduate school, Claire is more interested
in enjoying her money now than in saving for later.

"I'd much rather go skiing this weekend than spend it thinking
about my future," she says. Claire and I have been talking about various types of retirement plans for nearly four months now. We're
making progress, though. Although she still isn't wildly enthusiastic
about the idea of retirement planning, Claire *is* willing to listen. And
learn.

TAX-DEDUCTIBLE, TAX-DEFERRED, OR BOTH?

The retirement plans you have to choose from can be tax-deductible,
tax-deferred—or both. When the plan is tax-deductible, the money

that you contribute each year actually reduces your taxes for that year. Tax deferral is different. Deferral, as the word implies, means you are deferring or putting off paying taxes on income or capital gains in your retirement portfolio. Some retirement plans are "twofers," both tax-deductible and tax-deferred. This means you get to take a tax deduction every year on the amount of your contribution and you get to wait until you withdraw funds (when your tax bracket may be lower) to pay any tax on your portfolio's income earnings and capital gains.

Some retirement plans may be only tax-deferred and not tax-deductible. For example, some people can no longer deduct IRA contributions. Annuities (which can be an addendum to your retirement plan) are tax-deferred, but not tax-deductible. (IRAs and annuities are explained on pages 70 and 72.)

All retirement plans have different reporting requirements as well as different contribution limits. It's best to check with your CPA or pension plan consultant to make sure you comply with the regulations specific to your plan.

When you invest in a tax-deferred plan, the decisions you make will be motivated solely by the merits of the investment instead of by tax considerations. The up side to this is that if you want to take profits on stocks, you don't have to worry about paying capital gains tax now. However, if you suffer a loss, you don't get the tax break. This is why your tax-deferred investments should be concentrated in low-risk, "sleep at night" investments, with an additional inflation-fighting component.

Even if you can't deduct your retirement plan contribution, tax deferral still makes sense. No money is taken out for current taxes, more money remains in your portfolio, more money compounds, and more money grows.

Let me illustrate: Assuming a 9 percent rate of return and a 28 percent tax bracket, an *annual $2,000 tax-deferred* contribution to your IRA will be worth $33,121 after ten years. However, an *annual $2,000 taxable investment* after ten years will be worth only $21,161 after taxes are paid on the interest earned. The difference between these two returns is a whopping $11,960!

HOW DOES A RETIREMENT PLAN DIFFER FROM AN INVESTMENT?

Before I discuss the different types of retirement plans, let me make clear that these plans are *not* in and of themselves specific invest- ments. IRAs, Keoghs, 401(k)s, and other retirement plans are merely vehicles, or "umbrellas," offering a wide range of investment choices that can include mutual funds, stocks, bonds, CDs, money markets— almost any kind of investment you want.

People will call me up and ask, "What does your IRA pay? What's the return on your IRA?" These are not appropriate questions because an IRA or any other retirement plan doesn't yield anything. The yield or return on a retirement plan is a function of what it is invested in, which means that it's only going to do as well as the investments within it.

In any of your self-directed retirement plans, you can buy or sell whatever securities you want without any current tax consequences. This is important to remember because at various stages of your life you're going to want to reevaluate the different investments within these plans to determine whether or not they're still right for you.

STARTING AN IRA

An IRA is an individual retirement account. It's a type of retirement plan available to any worker under age 70½. You can contribute up to $2,000 a year, which may be fully, partially, or not at all tax- deductible. If you and your husband both work, you can each contrib- ute $2,000. If you don't work, your husband can establish his own $2,000 IRA and a spousal IRA with an additional contribution of up to $250 for you. *An IRA is not a specific investment. It is just a name for a type of retirement plan. Think of an IRA as an umbrella covering a wide range of investment choices.* For instance, your IRA may be in- vested in stocks, bonds, CDs, Treasuries, or mutual funds—it can be made up of any combination of investments that you want.

The big plus in an IRA is that your money grows tax-deferred. If you invest in a CD outside an IRA, you will be taxed on the interest earned. The same CD purchased inside an IRA will pay *no* current taxes on the interest earned.

Likewise, within your IRA you can sell a stock and take a profit, but you don't pay any capital gains tax, so the money you would have paid in taxes stays in your IRA and continues to grow. If you withdraw funds from your IRA before age 59½, you'll pay a 10 percent penalty on the amount withdrawn, which will also be taxed as ordinary income. You must start taking money out of your IRA shortly after you reach age 70½. If you don't, you'll pay a penalty as well.

It's important to note that laws governing IRAs are subject to change and are not etched in stone. Please consult with your tax adviser for specific updated information about IRA eligibility and deductibility.

LOOKING TO YOUR EMPLOYER: THE 401(K)

This is a retirement plan typically sponsored by a company, which may or may not be offered in conjunction with another retirement plan. It is essentially a salary-reduction program that allows you to contribute pretax income up to a specific dollar limit each year.

Having your retirement money deducted from your paycheck is a painless way to build your nest egg because the money is out of sight before it has a chance to reach your hands.

Let's assume that I receive a $1,000 paycheck. I can instruct my company to take $50 from this paycheck and put it in my 401(k) plan. This means that I will be taxed only on $950. It's as though I never got the extra $50, as it goes right into my retirement plan.

Sometimes a company will match your 401(k) contributions dollar for dollar. This means if you put away $7,000, your employer will put away an additional $7,000 for you. By matching funds, they are giving you a 100 percent return on your money. This is great because it's like getting free money! If this is your situation, you'll want to fund it to the maximum.

With some company retirement plans you can have total jurisdiction over the investments in your 401(k). This means you get to pick and choose. In other cases you may have to put your money in the company's own stock. Or your investment choices may be limited to a specific number of mutual funds. If so, be informed. Don't just check off boxes because they look interesting. If you have any questions or feel overwhelmed, look to the human resources director of your company for answers or further direction.

KEOGH PLAN

A Keogh is a retirement plan for the self-employed. You can make annual, tax-deductible contributions up to a maximum percentage of your income and to a maximum dollar amount.

If you establish a Keogh, you can have an IRA as well, although your IRA contribution may not be tax-deductible. You'll want to check with your tax adviser regarding contribution and deductibility provisions. Like an IRA, a Keogh is not a specific investment, but a type of retirement plan in which you can own any number of different investments.

SEP-IRAS, PROFIT SHARES, MONEY PURCHASE PLANS, AND DEFINED BENEFIT PLANS

These are different retirement plans with different and very specific eligibility and reporting requirements and contribution limits. Don't just make a wild guess as to which type of plan is best for you. Again, talk to your tax adviser or pension plan consultant before establishing one of these plans or participating in one. When you do identify the appropriate plan, try to contribute the maximum allowable by law each year. You will enjoy a current-year tax deduction, ongoing tax deferral, and a wonderful opportunity to secure your future.

ANNUITIES

Planning for your retirement through tax deferral can also be done by investing in annuities, which are sold through insurance companies and brokerages. Annuities are tax-deferred investments. An annuity is not actually a retirement plan. Think of an annuity as a nondeductible addition to your retirement savings. But, like retirement plans, annuity investments are tax-deferred, so earnings and capital gains are not subject to current taxation. There are also tax penalties for early withdrawals before age 59½.

Annuities are good addendums to retirement plans because there is no limitation on the amount of money you can invest. If you think you're going to need more money for retirement (which most people will) or if you're older and have less time to plan for retirement, an annuity can be an excellent investment.

There are two types of annuities. A fixed-rate annuity is almost like a CD in that it pays a specific interest rate each year. You can also invest in variable annuities, which allow you to select from among stock, bond, and money market portfolios. These portfolios are very much like mutual funds. This makes them riskier than fixed-rate annuities, but because of their growth potential, variable annuities can be excellent inflation hedges.

Until recently, annuities were considered very safe investments. But they are only as safe as the insurance companies that issue them. Given the failure or near failure of several insurers in recent years, you should investigate thoroughly and carefully before buying either type of annuity—fixed-rate or variable.

A good way to find out who's safe and who isn't is to check safety ratings with S&P, A. M. Best, and Weiss Research. Sometimes, but not always, the big-name insurance companies are your best bet. Even if you do find a high safety rating on the company you are interested in, check further—explore.

I suggest that instead of putting a great deal of your annuity money with one company, consider investing smaller amounts with two companies. I always tell my clients, "Why be a hero or a zero, when you can spread the risk?"

PLAYING IT SAFE

In a retirement portfolio I suggest a more conservative approach than I do with a regular investment portfolio. Why? Because there is no tax break for a loss. And when you lose money in a retirement plan you can't replace it because there is no way that it can "regenerate." For instance, if you invest $2,000 in your IRA in 1991 and you lose $500 on one of your investments, it can't be replaced. That money is not just gone, but the compounding aspect of the money is gone as well. The only way you'll ever make it back is if the other investments in your plan do terrifically well.

But if you're too conservative, inflation will erode the value of your portfolio. Your goal should be to strike a balance between safety (fixed-income investments) and inflation protection (growth investments).

Consider the mini-money triangle on page 58. In a retirement plan, you may want to eliminate entirely the very top of the triangle because the risk is too great. Again, the middle tier is for your growth/inflation protection investments, and the bottom tier of the triangle is for your very safe, fixed-income investments.

THE BIG STRETCH

If you are already investing in a company retirement plan like a 401(k) (which removes the money from your paycheck before you even see it), you may still want to have your own IRA. This means having the discipline to put this extra money aside. The investments in your self-directed IRA should strike a balance with the investments in your 401(k).

When clients tell me they work for company XYZ and I ask them what their pension fund is invested in, I have a good reason. I need to know where that money is because this will color my thinking in terms of what additional investments are needed. If you tell me you've got all Treasuries, we may start talking about stocks. If your 401(k) is heavily in stocks, we'll start investing in the bottom tier of the triangle with Treasuries, CDs, or money markets.

Always remember that when you're creating an investment strategy —whether for retirement or for your personal investment portfolio —everything is part of the same pie. The investments you have in your company retirement plan should complement what you have in your IRA and in your personal investment portfolio.

Some Retirement Investment Truisms

$ Your retirement plan is only as safe as the safety of your investments. There are no guarantees.

$ Annuities are not actually retirement plans, but they are tax-deferred and can be a good supplement to your retirement plan.

$ If your IRA is not tax-deductible, consult with your tax preparer before making further IRA contributions.

$ Retirement plans have early withdrawal penalties. In most cases if you withdraw funds before age 59½, you can expect a 10 percent penalty and you will be taxed on the money withdrawn. You may be able to borrow from your retirement plan, but check with your CPA or pension plan consultant first.

$ Most retirement plans require you to begin taking money out shortly after you reach 70½—or you'll be penalized.

$ You may also be penalized if you withdraw funds from an annuity before age 59½, *but* you don't have to start withdrawing funds after you reach age 70½. This allows you to extend the tax deferral.

$ Make sure you know how much you can contribute to your plan (or plans) each year. If you overfund, you could wind up paying a penalty.

$ When it comes to the ins and outs of retirement planning, check with your CPA, tax preparer, or pension plan consultant. In this area of investing, they are important members of your team.

When you're investing for retirement, you must think long term. This is why actively planning and monitoring your retirement portfolio is critical at *every stage of your life*. By doing this, you are not only taking charge of your financial future, you are securing your nest egg and preserving your wealth.

It's empowering to know where your money is, to understand how it's growing, and to know that because of the decisions you make, you'll be able to take care of yourself for the rest of your life. And there's a wonderful ripple effect when you're financially responsible. It's circular as it mirrors who you are: you're in control, you're calm, and you're confident. You can take care of yourself.

Why not start today?

WHAT'S THE BEST INVESTMENT TODAY?

There is no "best" investment today, tomorrow, or ever. The best investment is the investment that's best for you. Don't make the mistake of looking for that one get-rich-quick idea that's going to the moon! The best investment for you is one that makes sense, stays within your comfort level, and diversifies your portfolio. That's as good as it gets!

Secret #4...
Trust Your Warm Fuzzies: Taking Charge of Your Investments

Lisa came to me six months after her father died, leaving her an heiress at age twenty-eight. Her mother had died five years earlier, and Lisa, an only child, was the sole beneficiary of her father's multi-million-dollar estate. Fortunately her father had left the family finances in very capable hands: a wonderful attorney and a great CPA. Having worked through her grief, Lisa had finally reached that place inside that was telling her that it was not all right that she didn't have an overview of her investments.

Although it was very nice that she had these wonderful people taking care of her financial life, it just didn't feel okay anymore. She was a grown woman, and she wanted to understand *all* aspects of her life. *She wanted to be hands on with her investments.*

By making this decision, Lisa had taken her first investment step.

Fact Finding and Gathering Information: Disarming the Man with the Money

My first piece of advice for Lisa and for any woman trying to get involved with her financial life for the first time is to get an overview of the investments you already own *before you do anything else.* Even though you're probably eager to start investing, you can't just jump right in and start making decisions until you know what you already have—what you own and what you owe. This is why, before you do anything else, you must do your fact finding and information gathering. You are also going to have to form some sort of working relationship with the person who has been handling your money: your husband, your father, your CPA, your attorney . . .

You're probably wondering how you're going to enter this sacred male territory without getting your head shot off. Good question.

I suggest you be honest, direct, and realistic. Talk to your husband or to anyone else who has been managing your money and tell him point-blank:

"I'd like to get an overview of our financial picture. I haven't been involved up until now, and I feel it's important for both of us to be in the loop when it comes to our money. I'd like to gather some information before we start talking about our investments and debts. Right now, I think it's very overwhelming and confusing—so the more information and fact finding I can do, the better it will be for both of us."

Be prepared for some resistance and defensiveness. This is to be expected. It is extremely threatening to men when the women in their lives—whether it's their clients, their wives, or their daughters—want to take financial control all of a sudden. Their natural first response is going to be: "Why? Is something wrong? Don't you trust me? Don't you think I'm doing a good job?"

I don't fault men for feeling this way. It's logical. If you had been handling the finances all along and suddenly someone else stepped in and wanted to be a part of it, you probably wouldn't feel too comfortable, either.

This is why it is important that you validate his feelings with something like this: "You probably wonder where all of this is coming from, so let me explain that it has nothing to do with you. This is coming from a part of me that needs to grow up and take responsibility. I have no reason to second-guess what you're doing. I'd just like to get some information so that we can sit down and have a realistic conversation about our finances."

Next, allay his fears, telling him that it's been your choice not to be involved up till now, but now you *do* want to be involved. It has nothing to do with trusting him. Frankly, even if you do have reason to suspect that something is being mishandled, I wouldn't start waving red flags until you really know what's going on. And don't make negative comments like "I think you're handling this really badly." That would definitely not help you get the information you want.

A better approach is: "I'd just like to take a look at our finances. It's not that I doubt your abilities. It's just that I've been negligent, and I feel that it's important for me to be involved and understand what's what. Does this bother you? If it's a problem, let's discuss it so I can understand your feelings."

All of this can be said in a very nonthreatening way. If you don't get anywhere, you may have to get a bit more graphic to make your point, but do whatever it takes–even, for example:

"What if, God forbid, you get hit by a bus or have a heart attack or a stroke? How would I manage? What would happen to me? This is not about my taking over. This is about reality. Doesn't it make good common sense that both of us know where our money is and what it's doing for us?"

Yes, I know this sounds dramatic, but it does make sense. And if this did happen and you knew nothing about your finances, how would you manage? Where would you begin?

Doing What Feels Right

I was asking a very successful friend of mine how she makes decisions in life—both money decisions and life decisions. "It's simple," she said. "I have to feel the *warm fuzzies* about something." Now this is coming from a businesswoman who's got it all together.

I cracked up, laughing: "What do you mean, 'the warm fuzzies'?"

In all seriousness, my friend responded, "Typically, when I'm dealing with men, my husband included, if I make a personal or professional decision, I have to make it *sound* like it makes sense. Otherwise I'm not taken seriously. But in my heart of hearts, the reason that I'm making that decision is because I'm feeling the warm fuzzies."

She went on to explain, "You know how it feels when you put your feet in a pair of warm fuzzy slippers? It feels so good and it feels so right. That's where you want to have your feet. Well, it's the same thing in decision making. If it feels comfortable, if it feels right—that's where you belong; that's what you should do."

Understanding Your Warm Fuzzies

What are the warm fuzzies? I have no specific answer because they are hard to define and very intangible. They're gut-level feelings. Call it your sixth sense, your inner voice, or woman's intuition. Men seem to consider them nothing more than a hunch.

What makes up your warm fuzzies? All the things that you've ever seen, done, learned, and experienced blended together. A lot of it is based on previous experiences that somehow connect indirectly with what you feel at a given moment—it's then that the little bell goes off in your head. Think of it as the "Aha!" of the moment.

What's important is that these feelings are entirely valid. Although they can't always be explained, *they have to be respected.* The warm fuzzies are not irrational, negative emotions that prevent women from making sound financial decisions. These are positive, constructive emotions that come from deep down inside. These are the feelings that speak the loudest—if we'll only listen.

Intuition has always been regarded as a questionable and rather mysterious platform for decision making. But using it can enable you to see beyond the obvious as you look at the whole picture. It allows you to sense good versus bad character and honest versus dishonest intention. Traditionally men have considered it harmless as long as it is confined to the domestic aspects of life. But using it to make business decisions is like striking a hornet's nest with a broom!

Often a client will call to tell me that she has a bad feeling about one of her investments and thinks we ought to sell. One day a colleague of mine who had stopped by my office overheard one of these conversations and found it wildly amusing.

"Why is she selling?" he asked after I hung up.

"Because she has a bad feeling about the investment."

"Based on what?" he demanded.

"Based on a lack of warm fuzzies," I answered in my most nonchalant voice.

Dead silence. He walked out of my office shaking his head. End of conversation. But I could tell that he was dying to make fun of what he considered to be a ridiculous form of decision making. Warm fuzzies?!

What my colleague didn't know was that my client, Joanne, had at one point in her career worked as a banker at a major financial institution. She had often relied on her warm fuzzies for guidance when making important business decisions.

"I remember when my boss asked me to interview someone who had a triple-A résumé," Joanne told me once. "In fact, we joked that if he were a bond, he'd be a good investment. He told me he thought this fellow would be perfect for the position but wanted my opinion because this man would ultimately have to report to me. While his résumé was impressive, I sensed the opposite when we met, and I knew instantly that he'd never be able to cut it."

Joanne continued: "He wouldn't make eye contact with me, and although he was well dressed, I could tell by the way he spoke that he had very little self-confidence. The job he was after was geared for an aggressive, outgoing personality. It didn't matter how terrific his résumé was—he just didn't seem right to me."

When Joanne told her boss how she felt and tried to explain why, he ignored her feelings and hired the man anyway. Within six months this same man was fired. When her boss asked Joanne how she had foreseen that this guy would never work out, she simply answered in her best banker's voice, "I just knew. . . ."

Although her warm fuzzies were repeatedly ignored at the bank, they ultimately led her to the ownership of an extremely profitable executive search firm that interviews only the best and brightest executives. Some of the biggest companies in the world look to Joanne's firm to screen potential executives for their top management positions.

What made Joanne, already a successful banker, decide to take a chance on her new enterprise? Joanne explained, "I could feel it in my bones. Call it intuition, warm fuzzies, or whatever you like—I just felt that it would all come together. But being a businesswoman who had survived in the banking world, I knew that I would have to come up with concrete reasons if I wanted to line up the financial backers that I needed."

Common sense and her own hiring experiences told Joanne that her idea was a marketable service that high-profile companies needed. They could save time and money if potential executives were thoroughly screened before they turned up on a company's front door-step. Documenting this need gave substance to Joanne's warm fuzzies —and she used it to attract investors. Her track record as a successful banker didn't hurt, either!

We both get a good laugh when we think of how her warm fuzzies led her to create a business that also depends on warm fuzzies for its success. "When I interview an executive, the first thing I look for is intuitive ability . . . the rest of the job can be learned."

Listening to Your Warm Fuzzies
Can Help You Take Your First Investment Step

Intuition, sixth sense, gut feeling . . . all different ways to say warm fuzzies. Of course you've had them. Some examples:

"I always wake up a few minutes before my baby does, regardless of the time. Isn't that strange?"

"I wasn't surprised when the hospital called to tell me my mother had passed away. When I saw her last week, something told me I'd better say good-bye right then and there."

"I had a feeling I'd get that job. . . ."

"Something told me this blind date was going to be another Mr. Wrong."

And when it comes to money:

"I have a feeling that there is something very wrong with the fact that I'm a grown woman and know so little about money!"

This is the classic first comment I hear from many of my new clients. I breathe a sigh of relief. They're listening to their warm fuzzies directing them to take financial action. They are getting the message that it's not okay anymore for them not to know how to do money.

If this is you, what's the first thing you must change? Your lack of involvement.

Packaging Your Warm Fuzzies for Male Consumption

Once you've done your fact finding and information gathering, and you've asked and had answered every question, the next decision you must make is how hands on you really want to be. You've already opened up Pandora's box—do you want to close the lid or deal with what's inside?

If you feel good about the state of your finances—and your warm fuzzies combined with the facts are telling you that everything is being well managed—you may choose to leave it at that.

But if you want to be involved with your financial life (which is why I wrote this book and what I truly believe to be a necessity for every woman regardless of how good things seem at the moment), you may have to do some boat rocking. Perhaps you don't agree with certain investments that you've come across in your fact-finding venture. Maybe you believe in socially responsible investing and you don't like what company XYZ in your portfolio is doing to the environment. Or a $50,000 investment purchased two years ago is currently worth $25,000. . . .

The moment you speak up against an investment, consider yourself involved in the most positive sense. This means that with your input come the necessary changes in your habits and attitudes. And that's a good thing. You, too, should go over the monthly bank and brokerage statements. In fact, you should open every piece of investment information that comes in the mail. If you don't understand, ask for help. As you monitor your investments, continue to ask as many questions as you need until you completely understand.

If you want to be taken seriously, you have to develop financially responsible habits. This is where packaging your warm fuzzies for male consumption also comes into play. Instead of approaching an investment decision with "This doesn't feel right to me," find a concrete reason that will give substance to your warm fuzzy.

For example, instead of saying, "I really don't think that we should be so heavily invested in stocks. It just doesn't feel right," try this:

"I think our portfolio is off balance. We've got a lot of growth investments with these stocks, which means more risk. I think we should sell some of the "dogs," take our tax loss, and use the money to buy some income-producing bonds. What do you think?"

My point is that whenever you have a warm fuzzy about any investment, substantiate it in a way that the men in your life will understand.

Here's a good example: Felicia's husband has their money invested in CDs, short-term bonds, and other income-oriented investments. But the extra income they earn every month is not being reinvested—it's being spent! Suddenly Felicia is losing sleep at night because she's afraid that her husband's conservative investing and their extra spending will land them in the poorhouse before they hit fifty.

Why is Felicia losing sleep? Because her warm fuzzies are screaming very real bag lady nightmares at her.

Now if Felicia applies her common sense for a moment, she'll remember that she needs growth to offset inflation. Historically, one of the best hedges against inflation has been stocks.

Given Felicia's husband's temperament, she'll approach him with income stocks first—because there is both income and potential for growth. Once he's lived with owning income stocks for a while, he'll be more open-minded about owning growth stocks. Before Felicia knows it, like most good investors, her husband will have developed a balanced growth and income strategy.

Whenever you have a warm fuzzy, you should be able to figure out a way to substantiate it. Ask yourself these questions:

• Does what you're concerned about make good common sense to you? Does it make sense in terms of the other investments you own?

• What exactly is making you feel uncomfortable? Can you pinpoint the origin of your warm fuzzy?

• Does not being diversified have anything to do with it?

• What about discipline? Is this investment being held on to in the hope that you'll break even? Is your husband selling something that he just bought without even giving it a chance?

Now place all of your investments in the money triangle. Are they all in one tier? Are they all placed in the top, highly speculative tier? Are they allocated in the appropriate proportions for your age? (If you're forty-five you should have about 45 percent of your investments in income and the rest in growth. More about this in part 2.)

Ideally, one or both of these financial tools will help you find the trouble spot that substantiates your warm fuzzy.

If you are convinced that your warm fuzzy is accurate, even if you can't substantiate it, hold your ground. What's most important is that you never get talked out of a warm fuzzy. As a financial professional, I'm absolutely convinced that there are times when your warm fuzzies will be more on target than even the best professional advice.

Running the Numbers

One of the most impressive and on-target ways to substantiate your warm fuzzies to yourself and to others is to use simple mathematical equations. But more to the point, some investment decisions involve nothing more than a mathematical equation.

Your common sense and these simple math equations will help you believe in your warm fuzzies by showing you that you're not just experiencing some vague feeling—it's very real, and here's how you can prove it. This is also a big plus when packaging your warm fuzzies for male consumption. What man isn't impressed by numbers? It's a definite twofer—that is, it substantiates how you feel and also makes a lot of sense. Who can argue with numbers?

YOUR REAL RATE OF RETURN

Your real rate of return is what's left in your pocket after taxes and after inflation. The return on your investment is your starting point. From this you subtract your taxes and inflation.

What this means is that if you have a 10 percent return, you're not going to keep all of it. If it's taxable, and you're in a 37 percent combined bracket, you'll lose 37 percent to taxes right off the bat—of your 10 percent return you now have only 63 percent left. This translates into a return of 6.3 percent (10 x 63% = 6.3%). Now you have to subtract out for inflation, which varies from year to year. As I write this, inflation is a little under 4 percent, which is very low. Subtract this from 6.3 and you have just over 2 percent left. The 10 percent return you started out with translates into a real rate of return of just over 2 percent. It can be as little as 1 percent or even nothing if inflation is higher.

What Inflation Really Means in Terms of Your Warm Fuzzies and Your Real Rate of Return

If your warm fuzzies are telling you that certain investments aren't earning enough: "I'm not clear that we're making enough money here."

The argument you may get is, "Well, we're getting a 10 percent return."

To which you respond, "I'm not sure if that's really so great, and here's why. . . ." At this point, you figure out your real rate of return to substantiate your warm fuzzies.

Unfortunately, many investors forget to include inflation as a realistic part of their investment picture. This is a big mistake. To illustrate: At a 5 percent inflation rate, $100,000 loses a full $62,000 of its purchasing power in twenty years.

Remember Felicia's concern about her husband's conservative approach to investing and his spending the income that was earned on their investments? Her concern is unquestionably financially justified and very on target because of inflation.

To illustrate further, let's consider the price of apples per pound: In 1970 they were $.15, today they are about $.89, and the projected price in the year 2010 is a whopping $4.39! Inflation is a reality, and it isn't going away. And it very much affects the quality of your life.

So, substantiate your warm fuzzies, including your inflation fears, by figuring out your real rate of return:

- what it looks like you're getting

- minus the taxes you'll be paying

- minus the inflation factor

Once you've run these numbers, the reality will become apparent. You'll either know that your warm fuzzies were a false alarm, or you'll realize what kind of financial trouble you'll have in the future if you don't change your investment ways today.

Don't panic if the numbers do foreshadow future financial woes. Just as it is never too late to start investing, it's never too late to shift your investments or reconsider your strategy.

THE RULE OF 72

This is a nifty little equation that will determine the velocity of your money—in this case, how long it will take for your money to double. However, this equation does not take into account either taxes or inflation.

Take 72 and divide it by the return on your investment. Let's say you've got a 10 percent return on your investment. You would divide 72 by 10. This equals 7.2, which means that your money invested at a 10 percent return will take 7.2 years to double.

72 divided by 10% = 7.2
72 divided by the return on your investment = the
number of years it will take your money to double

You can also flip this equation around to figure out what kind of return you need to make your money double in X number of years. Let's assume that you are going to invest for five years. You take 72 and divide it by 5. This equals 14.4 percent. So if you are going to invest for five years, it will take a return of 14.4 percent on your investment to double your money.

72 divided by 5 = 14.4%
72 divided by the number of years invested = return on
your investment required to double your money

Again, remember that this does not take into account inflation or paying taxes on your investment.

This equation is useful in planning for a long-term financial goal because it shows you what is achievable and what isn't.

Let's say you have a nine-year-old child who will be going to college in eight years. You've got $20,000 to invest and you must double it in eight years. Take 72 and divide it by eight. This equals 9 percent. So if you are going to invest for eight years, it will take a return of 9 percent on an investment to double your money: to turn $20,000 into $40,000.

> **72 divided by 8 = 9%**
> **72 divided by 8 years invested = 9% return on your investment required to double your money**

Is this possible in today's economy? Yes, but you're going to have to consider owning some stocks because bonds won't quite do it.

The Rule of 72 is a good starting point when you're trying to determine how much you'll need to earn on your investment when you are working within a specific time frame to attain a specific financial goal.

TAXABLE OR TAX-FREE INVESTMENTS

Which way to go? One truism that you can apply here is that the higher your tax bracket, the more advantageous it will be for you to go with tax-free investments. For instance, investing in municipal bonds makes sense only for people whose after-tax yield on a tax-free bond or bond fund would be greater than the yield from a similar taxable investment.

The math is relatively simple: take your tax-free yield and divide it by 1 minus your combined tax bracket. That equals your taxable equivalent.

For example, let's say you live in Minnesota and your combined federal and state tax bracket is 37 percent. You're considering a tax-free bond that yields 6 percent. Take your tax-free yield of 6 percent and divide it by 1 minus 37 percent (which, as a decimal, is .37). Here is the equation:

6% divided by .63 = 9.52%
tax-free yield divided by (1 − .37) = taxable equivalent
    yield

The taxable equivalent yield is 9.52%. *That means to better the
6 percent yield on the tax-free investment, you would have to earn
more than 9.52 percent on an equivalent taxable investment.*

You can see how choosing between a tax-free and a taxable investment is nothing more than a simple mathematical equation.

An important point to remember is that when you make your cal-
culations you should make sure that the tax-free and taxable investments that you are comparing are of *similar quality and maturity.* For
instance, you'd want to compare a safe tax-free AAA municipal bond
to a safe taxable AAA corporate bond—not a risky junk bond.

Other People's Warm Fuzzies

The financial world is full of other people's advice, packaged in the
form of magazines, newsletters, columns in the business section of
your local newspaper, and television shows. Before following any of
the outside advice that is available, evaluate whether the "expert's"
approach is consistent with your own. What types of investments do
they favor, and what kinds of investors are they? Are they more buy
and hold, or are they traders? Growth investors or value investors?

Some market mavens are more aggressive than others. Some might
favor blue-chip stocks while others invest in small companies. My
point is that you should evaluate all advice carefully before applying it
to your own investments.

Just as your financial objectives should be consistent with the investments that you choose and with the advice of your financial advisers, so should anything you read dovetail with the strategy you already
have. If what you're reading contradicts the strategy and investment
approach that you really believe in, don't change what works for you.
But if you're intrigued and want to know more, check with your
financial advisers and get their opinions.

And be careful. Many newsletters are published by active traders, which means that they move in and out of investments very quickly. You're going to want to take their advice with a grain of salt because you are an investor, not a trader.

Also, evaluate their track record just as you would an actual investment. In the financial world, market mavens fall in and out of favor rapidly! They can be widely followed because they are right on the money for a couple of years. But then they make a wrong call on interest rates or the direction of stocks—and suddenly they are out of favor. This is why it's a good idea to diversify even your reading material. If you look at five different newsletters, you'll probably get five different opinions.

It would be a real mistake to become an ardent disciple of one of these gurus instead of sticking to the basics of common sense, comfort level, diversification, and discipline. Approach all advice as just that: advice. Information that you can consider. Believe me, no one has all the answers—no one has it all figured out.

Never forget that your warm fuzzies are an important and not-to-be-ignored part of your financial life. They are worth their weight in gold. Listen to them and trust them.

PART TWO

Getting Down
to Business:
Taking the
First Steps

WHAT DOES OWNING A STOCK REALLY MEAN?

When you own stock you own shares in a particular company. Even if you own only one share of AT&T stock, you actually own part of American Telephone and Telegraph. That means you get to participate in the company's growth when the stock price goes up, and you're entitled to "share income" when you receive dividends.

Secret #5 . . .
You Don't Have to
Shop 'til You Drop:
Understanding Your Choices

Picture this. It's five forty-five in the afternoon. You've put in a full day's work and now you're at the supermarket, trying to get your weekly shopping done. You zip through the aisles because you've promised your kids that you'll take them out for pizza at six, and you're a woman who keeps her promises. You sigh in relief as you reach the checkout counter—you have a good ten minutes to spare. You are about to empty your cart when you get this nagging feeling that you have forgotten something. Something is not right; you don't feel comfortable. As you stare down at your feet, you feel your big toe poking through the run in your stocking.

Panty hose! Now you have to buy panty hose!

You look at your cart in dismay. It's almost your turn. Should you leave your groceries and dash back for a pair of panty hose? The truth hits you hard. The cashier will have rung you up three times before you make it back. Then they'll be paging you over the intercom. Everyone behind you in line will think you ran out of money and ditched your cart. No one will save your place in line.

You have no choice. Reluctantly you turn your cart around and steer it to aisle nine—the home of L'eggs, Sheer Energy, No-Nonsense, Underalls, and all the rest. The choices are overwhelming. First, there's color to consider—you like beige, which is terrific in No-Nonsense but not so great in Sheer Energy. Ultimately the color and brand you get will be determined by the sizes available. Of course, you wear the most common size—medium. And comfort is every-thing.

Unfortunately, I have no answer to the panty hose problem. You've been there. You've experienced the drama. Who hasn't had her frozen foods thaw out while searching for the right pair of last-minute panty hose?

Personally, I find all shopping overwhelming because there are zillions of things to choose from. And I'm not alone. I know many women who are so intimidated by shopping that they use personal shoppers or go to boutiques where the choices are limited but at least manageable. Or they always shop at the same store because they know where everything is. This is why I'm amazed that the word *woman* has become synonymous with *shopping*.

The confusion many women feel about shopping is the same when it comes to making investment choices. Whether you are a novice investor or have many years of experience, there always seem to be a zillion investments to choose from. And to some extent this is true— at least in the generic sense.

When you open the business section of your local paper or *The Wall Street Journal,* pages and pages of different investments are listed. This includes everything from stocks to bonds to mutual funds to CDs to money markets—and just about everything in between.

Yes, there are hundreds of mutual funds to choose from, thousands of stocks to choose from, and thousands of bonds to choose from. *But you don't have to shop 'til you drop.* Your choices can be narrowed down with commonsense methods that will make your investment shopping a whole lot easier than you think.

The Many Roles Your Money Plays

It's important for you to understand that when you invest, your money takes on various roles. It can play the role of *principal* when you *invest* and come back to you as *interest, yield, capital gains, capital loss,* or *total return.* It all depends on how you invest it and what it does within the structure of the particular investment that you choose. These money role words that all define money in one form or another confuse you simply because they are unfamiliar to you and are often used incorrectly.

INVEST, INVESTMENTS, PRINCIPAL, AND RETURN

When you invest, the set sum of money you are "spending" on investments for future advantages and benefits is your principal (also called your capital). Your return is the money you get back from an investment, which may be in the form of interest income, yield, capital gain, or capital loss.

INTEREST, YIELD, FIXED-INCOME INVESTMENTS, AND MATURITY

Interest is the percentage that you will get back with your principal and along the way until your investment reaches maturity. Maturity is the date on which your principal is returned to you. Interest can be fixed or variable, depending on the investment. Top-quality fixed-income investments held to maturity (like bonds or CDs) do not typically affect your principal. They pay interest on your principal over a specified period of time.

For instance, if you invest $10,000 of principal in a fixed-income investment like a CD (certificate of deposit) at 5 percent for one year, at the end of the year your $10,000 principal has not increased or decreased. You are simply earning 5 percent interest for one year on $10,000—that's a return of $500 on your $10,000 principal.

Basically, the terms *interest* and *yield* are almost interchangeable. Interest is the actual money that is coming back to you, whereas yield is the percentage you are earning by investing your principal.

GROWTH INVESTMENTS, CAPITAL GAINS, AND CAPITAL LOSSES

Growth investments like stocks and real estate don't have a fixed rate of return. They're typically more volatile than fixed-income investments, which means they can and do go up and down. The good news is that you have the potential to make money. The bad news is that you risk losing money. So why take a chance with your principal? Because you believe you have a greater chance of making money than losing money.

If your investment goes up in value—if your principal is appreciating—you have a capital gain. If your investment goes down in value —if your principal is depreciating—you have a capital loss.

TOTAL RETURN

Your total return is the profit or loss on an investment, plus any interest you've earned on your principal. It's absolutely possible to be earning interest yet have a *negative* total return. Total return is critically important in evaluating the performance of an investment.

The Three Best Stores in Town: Cash, Stocks, and Bonds

When shopping, doesn't it make sense to understand which stores are the best and what they offer you? In the financial world, the best stores to shop in are the three major asset classes: cash and cash equivalents, stocks, and bonds.

CASH AND CASH EQUIVALENTS

Cash and cash equivalents are short-term financial instruments offered by banks and brokerage firms. They include checking accounts, savings accounts, money markets, short-term CDs, and Treasury bills. Your money is completely liquid and has no market risk. It means that you can touch and feel your money at any point in time and know that your principal is totally safe. And except for Treasury bills and CDs, you have no time constraint.

I would not include a five-year CD among cash and cash equivalents. It doesn't belong there because it's not completely liquid. With a five-year CD you have a five-year time constraint; you'll pay a penalty for early withdrawal if your CD is at a bank. And if you have a brokerage CD, you won't pay a penalty if you need to sell early—but you *are* vulnerable to interest-rate risk if rates go up.

CDs are certificates of deposit. They are often called "time deposits" because they have a specific maturity date. Their maturity can range from one month to several years, and they typically pay interest at a fixed rate with longer maturities paying higher rates than shorter maturities.

If you think interest rates are going up, one strategy is to put money into a short-term CD and then roll to a long-term CD when you can lock in a higher interest rate.

Most people think of CDs only in terms of banks. But there are actually two kinds of CDs: bank CDs and brokerage CDs. The difference in the two is that banks charge a penalty for early withdrawal and brokerages do not. If you need access to your CD money before maturity, brokerages sell your CD for you. As with bonds, the price that you get for your CD will depend on the direction of interest rates. If interest rates are up from when you bought your CD, you'll sell at a loss. If interest rates have gone down, you'll sell at a profit.

Brokerage CDs are exactly the same as bank CDs. In fact, brokerages buy their CDs from different banks throughout the country and then resell them to clients. Very few people know about brokerage CDs, but they are well worth looking into.

Cash and cash equivalents provide you with two things: safety and liquidity. Although your principal is not at risk, neither has it potential for growth. Obviously this is not the place to put all your investment dollars, but it *is* handy to have as a temporary home for your investment dollars until you decide what you want to do.

STOCKS

The second asset class is stocks. This includes everything from common stocks to preferred stocks, from penny stocks to blue chips, from over-the-counter (OTC) stocks to foreign issues.

When you're considering stocks as an asset class, you're typically interested in growth. You invest in common stocks because they have the greatest potential for growth, or "capital appreciation."

Growth stocks provide inflation protection for your portfolio. In fact, the primary reason to own stocks is to keep pace with inflation at least and, ideally, to outpace inflation. But remember: the more growth-oriented your investments, the riskier they are. And in many cases, rather than paying dividends, profits go back into the company to enhance its growth potential.

Although common stocks are excellent growth investments, preferred stocks are more income-oriented. The same is true of many utility stocks. Preferred stocks and utilities are often bought more for dividend income than for growth potential.

The question of whether or not to reinvest dividends can best be answered by using your common sense. If you need the additional income to live on, by all means use it. Don't reinvest it. If you don't need the extra income, reinvesting makes good sense.

When shopping for stocks you can pare down your choices by deciding whether you want stocks that are growth-oriented or income-oriented. If you're looking strictly for growth, then you're probably not going to be interested in preferred stocks or utilities. Conversely, if you're looking for income, you're not going to be shopping for most OTC stocks.

Stocks, Stockholder, Dividends, Preferred Stocks, and Common Stocks. When you invest in stock you actually own shares in a particular company and are considered a stockholder. Stock ownership entitles you to participate in the profits of the company, which means that when the company does well, the stockholders do well. This may entitle you to receive "share income," commonly known as dividends, on a quarterly basis—especially if you're investing in an income-oriented stock.

If the company you're investing in is growth-oriented, dividends, if any, are modest. The money you would have received in dividends goes back into the company to help finance further growth.

Stock ownership may be broken down into two types. You can be a preferred stock owner or a common stock owner.

Preferred stocks generally pay higher dividends and are less risky than common stocks. Preferred stock owners also receive dividends before they are paid to common stockholders. Preferred stocks can move up and down in price but are typically much less volatile than common stocks. The preferred stock is a kind of middle-of-the-road investment. You get more income than from common stock but less potential for growth.

Common stock owners take more risk, but they also have greater potential for reward because common stocks can grow more—and grow more rapidly—than preferred issues. Although they receive small, if any, dividends, if common stocks do well, they will outpace inflation. Remember that with common stock ownership there's always the chance that you could lose part, or all, of your investment. But if you stick mostly to blue-chip stocks, the odds are slim to none that you will lose all of your money.

Blue-Chip Stocks. Blue-chip stocks are perceived as the aristocrats of stocks, offered primarily by household-name, been-around-forever types of companies. These are the stocks of companies that are well established, well known, and well respected for their consistent ability to make money and pay dividends. But—a caution here—just because they are perceived as the best doesn't mean that they are. On the whole, though, they are excellent investments for long-term growth and income.

Penny Stocks. Penny stocks are the polar opposite of blue-chip stocks. These stocks represent little-known or unknown companies whose stocks sell for under a dollar a share. Usually they are extremely speculative. A few people become big winners with penny stocks, but most become big losers. They are often sold over the phone by less-than-reputable people who may have gotten your name from a mailing list or even from the phone book. This is the ultimate sucker bet for most investors.

What can I say? Penny stocks are not a pretty story. Yes, a couple of them started out in life selling for a few cents a share and ended up being worth big bucks, but most just fold up and die. Even if you invest only $2,000, it can be $2,000 gone forever, never to be heard from again. With the odds so decidedly against you, why bother?

Odd Lot and Round Lot. When you purchase less than one hundred shares of any stock, it's called an odd lot purchase, and it may cost you one-eighth of a point (12.5 cents) more per share. Sometimes it's cheaper to buy a round lot of stock, which is an even one hundred shares or multiple thereof.

Point. Points are measures of how stocks and bonds move up and down. One stock point is equal to $1.00. If your stock is up two points, it's up $2.00. If it's down half a point, it's down $.50. One bond point is equal to $10.00. So if your bond is down three points, it's down $30.00, and so on.

Equities. Equities are just another name for stocks. When you have equities in your portfolio, you have stocks in your portfolio.

BONDS

The third asset class that you'll be shopping in is bonds, or "fixed income." This includes a broad spectrum of bonds, from the most conservative Treasuries to the riskiest high-yield junk bonds (which you should avoid like the plague).

You shop for bonds when you're looking for income. Bonds held to maturity have no growth potential or inflation protection. As the term *fixed income* implies, bonds generally have a fixed rate of return. If you buy a bond with a 6 percent coupon, you earn 6 percent interest. If interest rates go higher, you still earn only 6 percent. Period. End of story. You can see how bonds held to maturity provide no growth at all. What you get from bonds is steady, predictable income.

Bonds. Whereas with stocks you own, with bonds you loan—to the U.S. government, to corporations, or to municipalities, for example. The safest bonds are U.S. government bonds (commonly called "Treasuries"), which are full faith and credit obligations of the U.S. government. The riskiest bonds are high-yield "junk" corporates or municipals. Junk bonds are issued by less creditworthy companies and municipalities, whose ability to pay interest or repay principal is somehow questionable. Any bond with the name "junk" attached to it means high risk, but it can also mean an extremely high rate of return if it works out—or a substantial loss of principal if it doesn't.

Many people find bonds confusing, so let me explain the different components of a bond first. Most bonds have a par value (or face value) of $1,000 per bond, which never changes; a coupon rate (or nominal rate), which is the interest rate you are paid semiannually until it matures; and a maturity date, which is when you are paid par value for each bond that you own. If you buy ten bonds, you will receive semiannual interest payments based on the bonds' coupon rate and $10,000 principal when they mature.

I think where bonds get tricky is in understanding that when you buy a bond you will not necessarily pay par ($1,000) for it. And if you have to sell a bond before it reaches maturity, you may get more or less than you paid for it. Why? Because although the par value never changes, the actual price of a bond moves up or down in the opposite direction of interest rates.

If interest rates have gone down since you bought your bond, the value of your bond has gone up. It's worth more now, which means you'll make a profit if you decide to sell it instead of holding it to maturity. Conversely, if interest rates have gone up, the value of your bond has gone down. If you need to sell your bond, it will be at a loss because it's worth less now than when you bought it.

Remember, though, that if you buy fixed-rate bonds at any time and hold them to maturity, your bonds will not be affected by the direction of interest rates one way or the other. When you buy them, you lock in your coupon rate, which specifies the interest you'll receive. When your bonds mature, you'll be paid par value ($1,000) for each bond that you own.

Zero-Coupon Bonds. A zero-coupon bond, as the name implies, is a bond that pays no interest—it has a zero percent coupon rate. A zero can be a government, municipal, or corporate bond. Although its par value is typically $1,000, which is what you'll receive when it matures, you buy it at a discount—anywhere from under $100 to over $900 a bond, depending on the number of years until maturity. Zero-coupon bonds are good investments for those of you who do not need current income but do need to plan for a future event like retirement or your children's college education. One of the advantages of having zero coupons in your portfolio is that you know in advance exactly what they will grow to be worth at maturity.

Treasuries and Agencies. Investing in Treasuries means that you are loaning money to the U.S. government. Investing in agencies (Ginnie

Mae, Freddie Mac, Fannie Mae, and their kin) means that you are loaning money to an agency of the U.S. government (Government National Mortgage Association, Federal Home Loan Bank, Federal National Mortgage Association, and so on). U.S. government bonds are considered the ultimate in safety because they are backed by the full faith and credit of the U.S. government. Agencies are one step removed in safety because, with the exception of Ginnie Maes (see next entry), they're backed by the agencies themselves rather than by the U.S. government directly.

Treasury bills, notes, and bonds are marketable securities and can be bought and sold through brokerage houses and other financial institutions. You don't have to hold them to maturity, and there are no penalties per se for selling them before maturity.

But as with all bonds, the price of a Treasury security *will* move up and down inversely with interest rates. If interest rates have moved down when you want to sell, you'll sell at a profit. If interest rates have gone up when want to sell, you'll sell at a loss.

Treasury bills, unlike notes and bonds, are sold at a discount and do not pay interest. At maturity you will receive full face value, so your return is the difference between what you paid for the Treasury and its face value at maturity. Treasury bills have maturities of one year or less. One-year Treasury bills are a widely used benchmark for comparing the relative safety and performance of alternative investments.

Treasury notes have maturities of one to ten years; Treasury bonds have maturities of ten years and more. Notes and bonds pay interest every six months and return your principal at maturity.

Ginnie Maes (GNMA). Ginnie Mae is an acronym for Government National Mortgage Association. To most investors, the GNMA is the best known of the U.S. government agencies. GNMA purchases loans from banks and repackages them as pooled mortgage obligations. These pools are then resold to investors as fully taxable bonds that generally pay higher interest than Treasuries. They are available in minimum denominations of $25,000, which is why many people invest in them through mutual funds, which have lower minimum investment requirements.

As an investor it is important to understand that returns on your

Ginnie Mae investment include interest payments as well as partial return of your own principal as people either pay off or refinance their mortgage loans. A Ginnie Mae *does* have a specific maturity date, but, again, as people refinance, you will be getting back part of your principal along the way, rather than in one lump sum at maturity.

When investing in Ginnie Maes, many investors mistakenly think, Okay, I invested $25,000. I'll get interest along the way, and when it matures I'll get back my $25,000 principal." *Wrong*. What most people don't realize is that what they're getting back along the way is not strictly interest income. Part of it is their principal, too. What a shock they have when their investment matures and they get only part of their principal back—especially if they've been using the payments they've received as income instead of saving or reinvesting the principal portion.

Another problem with investing in Ginnie Maes is that if interest rates come down dramatically and many people repay their loans, you could end up getting a large chunk of your own principal back at a time when you least want it—when interest rates are really low and you're forced to reinvest at much lower rates.

Corporate Bonds. When you invest in corporate bonds, you are loaning money to a corporation. Some corporations are solid financially, and their bonds are considered investment grade (rated AAA, AA, A, or BBB) and high quality. Less creditworthy corporations issue lower-rated (BB or lower), higher-yielding bonds to compensate you for the risk you are taking. Your biggest risk is credit risk, especially the possibility of default (inability to repay your principal at maturity). Corporate bonds pay fully taxable interest every six months. In my opinion, buying even high-quality corporates makes sense only if they yield significantly more than Treasuries or agencies with comparable maturities.

Municipal Bonds. States, cities, schools, water districts, hospitals, housing authorities, even sewer projects, can issue municipal bonds. Although munis enjoy a general reputation for safety, each bond must be evaluated on its own merits. As with all bonds, you should be most concerned about the issuer's ability to pay interest and repay principal. Interest payments on munis are federally tax-free and are also state tax-free to residents of the state in which they are issued.

International Bonds. Sometimes interest rates are higher overseas than in the United States, so investors buy foreign government bonds instead of (or in addition to) Treasuries. International bonds have the same risks as domestic bonds *plus* currency risk. It's good news for you if the U.S. dollar weakens against the foreign currency in which your bond is denominated. If the U.S. dollar gets stronger, you could end up with an unpleasant surprise. Remember the concept of total return. You could be getting a higher yield in an international bond, but if you're losing principal, be on guard.

Making Your Shopping List

Within these three asset classes—cash, stocks, and bonds—you will do your shopping. If you are a new investor without a portfolio, you're going to examine all three asset classes. In the money triangle on page 58, you'll notice that these three asset classes make up the first and second tiers of the triangle. It is in these two tiers that almost all conservative, commonsense investors do their shopping.

Of course, it's very difficult to shop for anything unless you know what you need. With this knowledge you can make your list. Defining your financial objectives in advance and prioritizing them to the best of your ability is the best way to avoid shopping 'til you drop. Whether you're a new investor or a seasoned investor, the following questions should help you make your list:

• What are your specific short-term and long-term financial goals? Buying a new house in five years? Retiring in fifteen years?

• What kinds of investments do you already own? How comfortable are you with these investments?

• How much risk are you prepared to take to achieve your financial goals?

- For what period of time are you willing to invest?

- What's most important to you? Safety? Income? Or growth?

If growth is most important to you, the asset class you'll be shopping in is stocks.

If you need income and don't want to take much risk, then you'll be shopping for bonds. If you want no risk, stick to Treasuries.

If you need income and don't mind taking some risk in exchange for potential growth, you'll be shopping for preferred stocks—and maybe some utilities.

From time to time you may need to shop for cash or cash equivalents for safety or to meet short-term needs. Let's say you're saving up for a new car that you're going to be buying in the near future. Your choices? You could put your money in a savings account, a money market, or in a short-term CD or T-bill. You'll need to know exactly how much time you have before the money is needed, then shop for the cash equivalent that pays the highest interest but is completely safe. If your time frame for investments is at least one to two years or longer, you may want to shop for an intermediate-term CD or T-bill to be used in conjunction with a savings or money market account.

My client Jody, twenty-two, hoped to continue on to graduate school for her master's in taxation after completing college with a bachelor of science in business administration. But she didn't have the tuition money and didn't want to take on another student loan or turn to her parents for help yet again.

Jody decided on a five-year plan. She took a job as a junior accountant and began studying for the CPA exam. During the next five years her plan was to pass the exam, satisfy the experience requirement necessary to become licensed, and save as much as possible of her $28,000-per-year salary for graduate school.

With her professional and financial objectives clearly defined, Jody set out to achieve her goals. She began by investing her $3,000 of graduation money—all gifts from relatives—in a CD maturing in exactly five years.

Each month Jody added to her investment nest egg by depositing into a separate interest-bearing savings account money saved from her paycheck. At the end of year one Jody purchased a four-year CD with her savings; at the end of year two she bought a three-year CD.

Now almost three years into her five-year plan, Jody has passed the CPA exam and has recently received a salary increase and a substantial cash bonus. It looks as if she will enter graduate school in the near future, perhaps even sooner than she had originally planned.

Shopping for cash or cash equivalents—either alone or in conjunction with another investment—may not seem too exciting, but for many investors it's exactly the right approach.

My client Eleanor was about to remodel her home and had gotten an equity line of credit from her bank. Because the contractors were delayed, she needed a safe place to put this money for at least three months and no longer than six months. Eleanor loves the stock market, so she called to ask me which stocks she should put this money into for the next three to six months.

Eleanor was definitely shopping at the wrong store. I had her revisit her financial objectives. What did she want this particular sum of money to do for her? She told me: "Well, I need it to remodel my home, and it's going to take every penny that the bank loaned me to do the job. But it's going to be three to six months before the contractors can start, so I'd like to put it in something where it can grow during this time. This is why I think stocks would be good."

I told Eleanor that stocks were inappropriate because she needed to keep this money safe. She had made it very clear that she would need all of it in a short period of time for remodeling. She couldn't afford to lose any of it. It was earmarked for a specific purpose. Even though she liked stocks, we would have to cross them off her shopping list because of the time frame involved, her need for liquidity, and her need for safety.

The only asset class she could shop in would be cash and cash equivalents. This was the only investment "store" appropriate to her needs. What I said to her was: "Here is what a money market is yielding, here is what three- and six-month Treasuries are yielding, here are what three- and six-month CDs are yielding."

In planning for her specific needs in this way, Eleanor would not have to shop 'til she drops—she would, in fact, be shopping at one store only: the store that sells cash and cash equivalents.

By revisiting her investment objective, Eleanor prevented herself from making what could have been a terrible mistake. Had she gone ahead with stocks, she might have had a real problem if her stocks were down at the time she needed to sell to get the money for the contractors.

Eleanor's story makes an important point when it comes to financial planning: *Make sure your financial objectives are consistent with the asset class in which you're shopping.*

Window-Shopping

It's interesting how a client will tell me her investment objectives are safety and income and in the next breath ask me about an aggressive growth stock. This "window-shopping" happens all the time.

Sharon tells me that she is about to retire and doesn't want to take much risk. In addition to her pension benefit and Social Security income, she'll need extra money to live on. I suggest shopping for an income portfolio, which includes Treasuries, insured tax-free bonds, and some utility stocks.

Then, out of the blue, in true window-shopper fashion, she asks: "What do you think of XYZ stock? A lot of people at work are talking about it being the next *hot* investment!" Now XYZ might be a potentially wonderful investment, but discussing it is nothing more than window-shopping because Sharon can't afford the risk that comes with owning this very aggressive high flyer.

I remind her: "You've already determined that your objectives are safety and income. You don't have the capital or the risk tolerance to buy this stock. You need income-oriented investments because you need the extra money they will provide for you to live on."

Don't get me wrong. Window-shopping can be fun. But it can really throw you off track and can end up costing you far more than the fun is worth. If you're well on your way to meeting your financial objectives and you've got the "play" money, then great—go for it! But don't let window-shopping get in the way of serious investing.

For some of my clients who tend to window-shop I share an analogy related to clothes shopping.

If you need business clothes, you don't shop in the evening wear department. As you're walking out of the store with your entire business outfit already in hand, if you stop by evening wear and see a stunning cocktail dress that really catches your eye, there's nothing wrong with buying it. *If* you have the extra money. But if you've allocated your money for business clothes and still need to buy a skirt, don't buy that perfect little evening dress no matter how terrific it is.

Packaging Your Purchases

Now that we've unwrapped the three basic asset classes, let's talk about packaged products—specifically, mutual funds.

MUTUAL FUNDS

A mutual fund is a way to invest in a professionally managed portfolio where many investors' dollars are pooled together. The investment dollars can be pooled together in an *income fund,* which consists of bonds; in a *growth fund,* which consists of stocks; in a *balanced fund,* which is a mix of stocks and bonds—and you can even go abroad with an *international* or *global fund.*

This is a good investment for those of you who have a small amount to invest, because the pooling of dollars allows for a wide range of diversification. For instance, if you have $10,000 to invest, you will not be able to buy a well-diversified portfolio of stocks. But with the same $10,000 you can buy shares in a mutual fund and get a lot of diversification. However, you don't get to make investment decisions on a day-to-day basis. A professional fund manager does all of the buying and selling and is the hands-on decision maker.

So the up side of owning a mutual fund is that you can get a lot of diversification for very little money. The down side is that the fund manager calls the shots, and if anything obscures his financial vision, you could lose money and see red.

Shopping for a Mutual Fund

While shopping for the right mutual fund, here are some tips for picking and choosing, as well as questions you should ask:

• How long has the fund been around? You don't want to invest in a brand-new fund because you don't have any way to track its performance. If it did very well last year, so what? You need to know what it did five and even ten years ago, when maybe the markets weren't so wonderful.

• Find out who the fund manager is and how long he or she has been around. This is very important because, as I said before, this is the person who will be calling the shots. A well-known mutual fund was headed by a top manager for years. He left and a new manager took over and then two years later was replaced by yet another manager. When the five-year track record of this fund was examined, it was important to remember that the new manager coming in had nothing to do with the previous track record. You couldn't judge his potential by this fund's past performance. That is why it is vital that you know who the fund manager is and how long he or she has been managing the fund.

• Find out how frequently the fund you're interested in "turns over" its portfolio. Is it a buy and hold approach or more of an active trading approach?

• If you're looking at a stock mutual fund, you'll want to know the type of stock the fund invests in. If it's a blue-chip mutual fund, you know it invests primarily in large, household-name companies.

• Whether it's a blue-chip mutual fund or another type of stock fund, make sure you ask what the top ten stock holdings are. Six months from now this can change because of the trading that is likely to occur within the portfolio, but at least you'll get a good idea of the type of stocks they look at. You'll also get a sense of their vantage point and the approach they take to stock selection.

If you are shopping for a bond mutual fund, you'll want to ask these questions:

• What is the credit quality or the average rating of the bonds in the portfolio?

• What is the average maturity of the portfolio? Let's assume the average maturity of Bond Mutual Fund A is thirty years. This means that it will be a lot more volatile than a portfolio holding three-year bonds. Yields are usually higher with longer maturities, but so is risk.

• Find out the yield on the fund, but also check the total return. Total return means that even though you are getting a wonderfully high yield, you may be losing part of your principal at the same time. If you paid $10 a share for a bond mutual fund, and it is now $9 a share, you've lost 10 percent of your principal. If you're getting a 10 percent yield, you're just breaking even.

• Finally, find out what the fund's yield and total return have been over the last year and over the last five and ten years. This will reflect what it has been yielding, as well as what has happened to the principal. If you're told that the yield on a bond fund was 9 percent last year and the total return was 7 percent, then 2 percent of the principal was lost. The total return can be higher or lower than the yield.

Total return is a much better indicator of the overall performance of the fund than yield figures alone. It not only tells you what your principal earned, it also shows whether actual dollars increased or decreased.

Why go through all of this before investing in a mutual fund when there is a fund manager making all the decisions? Because the mutual fund that you invest in, whether it is a stock, bond, or balanced fund, should be in sync with your investment objectives. This takes us back to my original premise that you don't have to shop 'til you drop if you define your financial objectives in advance and make an appropriate shopping list.

If you choose mutual funds as your primary investment vehicles, don't invest all your money in just one fund. Always diversify. Remember, a mutual fund's performance is only as good as the performance of the fund's manager. Some people sink as much as $500,000 into one mutual fund—a real mistake, in my opinion. These investors have put an awful lot of eggs in one basket.

Personally, I wouldn't put more than $50,000 in any one mutual fund. But don't be afraid to invest $50,000 in one fund unless that's all the money you've got to invest. Again, it comes back to diversifying with what you have and applying your common sense.

Of course, the flip side of this is that someone with $10,000 to invest shouldn't own five different mutual funds. Two maybe, but not five. Don't diversify yourself to the point of absurdity.

MONEY MARKET MUTUAL FUNDS

These are funds that buy and sell *short-term* financial instruments. Normally they keep a stable dollar price of $1 per share. The interest rate changes every day because the investments are so short term. You can use money market funds as a checking account—the bonus is that you'll get interest and have check writing privileges, too. You can pay your bills out of this account.

Most banks, brokerages, and mutual fund companies offer money market funds. It's a good place to "park" your cash and earn interest at the same time. Think of it as a cash place.

Some people use money market funds as the cash part of their portfolio. For example, let's say that you have $100,000 to invest. You may want to hold $20,000 in cash while you wait to decide about buying a particular investment. While you're deciding, your $20,000 is collecting interest, so it's working for you in the meantime, too.

STOCK MUTUAL FUNDS

Buying shares in a stock mutual fund means that you are investing in a portfolio of stocks. Stock mutual funds come in all shapes and sizes from blue-chip funds to small company funds to sector funds that invest only in one industry (like health care). Stock funds can range from low risk to high risk depending on the types of stocks they hold.

BOND MUTUAL FUNDS

Bond mutual funds can be government bond funds holding only Treasuries or agencies, corporate bond funds, municipal bond funds, and so forth. Don't just compare yields when you choose a bond fund. Compare quality and maturity, too. Short-term, higher-rated bond funds pay less but offer more safety.

BALANCED FUNDS

These funds contain both stocks and bonds, looking for both growth and income. It's a way of almost splitting the difference between a stock fund and a bond fund and can be a good middle ground for beginning investors.

GLOBAL AND INTERNATIONAL FUNDS

International funds can invest anywhere outside the United States; global funds are free to invest in both U.S. *and* foreign securities. These are good ways to own foreign stocks and bonds and to let a fund manager who is an expert in the overseas markets manage these investments for you.

SOCIALLY RESPONSIBLE FUNDS

Investors who want to put their money where their heart is can look to stock and bond mutual funds that own only specially screened investments ranging from stocks of environmentally friendly companies to municipal bonds issued to further education and health care. Many of these funds have performed excellently, proving that you can do good *and* do well at the same time.

One of the big pluses of mutual funds is that they have the resources that most individual investors don't have to research companies thoroughly. If you believe in socially responsible investing, *socially responsible mutual funds* may be exactly right for you. They have the capacity to investigate potential investments with a fine-tooth comb to ensure that they are consistent with the restrictions imposed on these funds.

Some socially responsible funds have very broad screens while others have narrower ones. Some specifically screen out environmentally unfriendly companies; others don't. Some funds extend their screens all the way to equal opportunity hiring practices.

If you're interested in a particular socially responsible mutual fund, find out exactly what this fund screens for. For instance, if you don't want to own any of the "sin" stocks (gambling, alcohol, or tobacco), make sure they screen for these. If you disapprove of animal testing, make sure this yardstick is included.

Custom Tailoring: Creating Your Own Portfolio

With stocks and bonds there are two ways to shop: do it yourself or invest with a mutual fund or professional money manager.

A lot of the shopping information at the beginning of this chapter can easily be applied to stocks. But creating a well-diversified bond portfolio can be more complicated. If you are going to assemble a bond portfolio yourself, you'll need some specific information from the start. Again, this will help you winnow out inappropriate choices so your bond shopping doesn't overwhelm you.

First of all, do you want tax-free or taxable bonds? This is a simple case of math—no guesswork involved. You may want to consult your accountant or tax preparer to help you decide which works best for you.

If you want completely tax-free bonds, then you can forget about Treasuries, agencies, foreign bonds, and corporate bonds. You're going to have to stick with municipal bonds . . . period. So already you've pared down your shopping list from that big universe of bonds to *just* municipal bonds because they are the only tax-free bonds available.

If you decide on taxable bonds, exactly the opposite is true, which means you can consider every kind of bond *except* municipal bonds.

If you are only comfortable owning Treasuries because of their safety, that's fine. But if you need a 10 percent return and Treasuries yield 7 percent, you're going to have to decide which is more important to you—absolute safety or income. Although your comfort level may dictate that you want Treasuries, you may have to kiss them good-bye because you need more income than they can provide.

This is a key point. You have to list investment objectives by priority when you're shopping.

If you do decide to buy bonds that will provide you with more income, you need to recognize that there is some risk involved. Although you will not have the safety of Treasuries, you *will* get the income that you need. Just remember that the higher the yield, the higher the risk.

If you tell me that the rate of return you need is higher than what Treasuries *or* agencies yield, then we may have to look only at corporate bonds.

Your shopping list has gone from a universe of bonds to a selection of corporate bonds. We won't shop for Treasuries or agencies because you can't live on the income they provide. Yes, it's really this simple to pare down your choices.

You Can't Have It Both Ways

I ask clients very specific questions: "How much income do you need each month? Write down the actual dollar figure. How much of this amount is already accounted for by your salary, an inheritance, child support, alimony, and so on? How much is the shortfall that we need to make up?"

Phyllis, for example, needed $750 extra a month for the next three years. She had $100,000 to invest. I sat down with my calculator to figure out what rate of return was necessary to meet her needs. By doing this, I also figured out what I could shop for. In Phyllis's case, simple arithmetic told me that she needed a 9 percent return at a time when three-year Treasuries were yielding just under 6 percent. This is a problem many clients have. They want safety, but they need income. Unfortunately, as in many areas of life, you can't have it both ways.

However, if Phyllis had told me that she could make do with $500 a month because she needed safety even more than she needed the extra income, we could have discussed Treasuries. Her choice was between taking some risk or settling for less income. She chose safety first.

In many ways this is the same approach you take when shopping for stocks: determine your objectives, list them by priority because you can't have it all, and then pare down your choices.

Angela, twenty-eight, tells me she needs a 25 percent annual return on her stocks so she can afford to buy her dream house in ten years. She wants conservative blue-chip stocks, however. At this point I have to tell her that although I understand her objective, in order to get a 25 percent return she will have to consider smaller, more aggressive companies. She needs to take more risk and hope for a higher reward.

In the financial markets it always comes down to risk versus reward . . . or safety versus return . . . or growth versus income.

Making It Happen

Let's assume you need a fair amount of taxable income, so now you've crossed many choices off your shopping list. You are finally ready to put together your own bond portfolio. You've reconciled yourself to taking the risk that is part and parcel of owning corporate bonds because you need the income. After you've put together your portfolio of corporate bonds, you apply your common sense.

This means that you don't put all your money in one bond or in bonds issued only by automobile companies, for example. Instead, you would also buy some utility bonds, some telephone company bonds, and so on. My point is for you to understand the need to diversify across different industry lines, just as you do when selecting stocks.

Next, apply your comfort level, which means respecting your risk tolerance. Do you want investment-grade bonds? Only AAA bonds? Or are you willing to buy an A-rated bond, which carries more risk but generally offers more income?

At this point, if you don't have the time to do this planning on your own or the dollars to create a well-diversified bond portfolio, look to bond mutual funds.

If you decide to continue by yourself, know that when you are constructing a bond portfolio it's good to take a "laddering" approach. This means that you'll own different bonds with different maturities. You'll want to buy bonds that mature in one year, three years, five years, and so on.

If you've decided to go with bond mutual funds, you should know that they have no finite maturity date. This is very important to under-stand.

Let's assume that you own a portfolio of individual bonds. If you hold them until maturity, and they're good-quality bonds, you're going to get your principal back.

But unlike individual bonds, a bond mutual fund has *no* guarantee that dollars *in* will equal dollars *out*—and there is no specific maturity date when your principal is returned to you intact.

There are two dynamics going on here. If you hold an individual bond, you know that you'll get your principal back when the bond matures. In a bond mutual fund, though, most bonds aren't held to maturity because the fund manager actively trades them—sometimes at a profit, sometimes at a loss.

You can see how owning a bond mutual fund can mean higher risk than owning individual bonds. And the longer the average maturity on the bonds in a mutual fund, the more risk there is due to the volatility in longer maturities. *But* if interest rates drop, you'll make more money in a long-term bond mutual fund than in a short-term fund. Again, risk versus reward.

Income versus Principal

Some investors, particularly retirees, have the attitude that that they need as much income as possible now. As far as they're concerned, if the principal goes down, it just means their kids will inherit less. This is valid if it works for you. Some people are more concerned with current income than preservation of principal.

If this is your situation, obviously you are looking for the highest yield you can get. But that still doesn't mean you should chase junk bonds!

There are also investors who feel just the opposite. They will forgo income to preserve their principal, even if it means cutting back on their life-style.

There is no right or wrong here. It all goes back to your objectives, how you rank them, and how well disciplined you are in the follow-through.

Bread, Butter, and Truffles

Although we've focused on the major asset classes and discussed mutual funds at length, there are other investments we haven't talked about much, probably because I think of them as ribbons and bows —the trimmings. Or to use a food analogy, they're not the bread and butter of investing—they're the things we nibble on that aren't very filling. And sometimes don't even taste very good.

Gold and other precious metals, for example, used to provide good inflation protection because precious metals kept pace with—and often outpaced—inflation. But this isn't true anymore. You can get much better inflation protection with growth stocks these days.

Artwork and collectibles, like limited plate editions, doll collections, and so on, *can* be good inflation hedges and can provide good growth potential. The extra plus is that they are certainly more aesthetically pleasing than a stock certificate. One problem is that many investors form sentimental attachments to their collectibles. That makes it difficult to sell and take profits. There's nothing wrong with this. To sell or not to sell is up to you, but do remember why you invested in the first place.

COLLECTIBLES

Collectibles can include artwork, coins, stamps, porcelain, antique dolls, baseball cards, rare books, you name it. Collectibles are bought in the hope that they will appreciate in value and outpace inflation. A good collectible can be a very good inflation hedge. There is also the aesthetic appeal of collectibles —they are certainly much nicer to look at than a stock certificate. Unfortunately, with collectibles there is a lot of room for fraud. You have to know and research the value of what you're collecting thoroughly, as well as the background and integrity of the person from whom you're buying.

Collectibles can become an interesting part of your portfolio, adding diversification and profit. Collectibles traditionally do well during periods of high inflation, but during a recession prices will likely be down and you may have to stay tuned for quite a while before they rebound.

If you have the extra money to shop for precious metals, artwork, or collectibles, that's fine. My main concern is that you take care of the bread and butter before you buy the truffles. If you need growth and income, stick with growth and income investments because this is your bread and butter. Truffles are extras. You can live without them quite comfortably, and most people don't even like the way they taste!

Using Personal Shoppers

You can use financial advisers to be your personal shoppers. (In Secret #7 you'll learn about the different types of advisers and how to choose the right ones.) Ask them what they invest in for income. What do they shop for if they need growth? These are important questions because we all have our own opinions.

For me, income means bonds. Growth means stocks. It's that simple. But I don't expect everyone to agree with me. I operate this way because my comfort level is about keeping things simple. I don't like all the bells and whistles, the bows and fancy trimmings in which many investments are packaged. Does this mean that there aren't other solutions? No. But it is how I'm most comfortable investing. It works for me.

I choose what I feel are appropriate, commonsense investments. Sure, there are lots of other choices—but why not keep it simple? I may choose a mutual fund because it's a great long-term performer and I like the types of stocks it invests in. It fits my objectives—so why should I look elsewhere?

For me, shopping for investments is like shopping for shoes. You go to the shoe store and tell the salesperson that you need beige pumps with low heels and a wide toe. You've already narrowed down the salesperson's choices so he won't bring you every beige pump in stock—anything with pointed toes and high heels is definitely out.

Let's say that the first pair of beige pumps you try on feels and looks great. Why do you need to try on anything else? If you want to try on five more pairs, go ahead. But why bother if the first pair feels comfortable and works just fine? You've met your objective because you've defined your needs.

This is how your financial advisers are able to help you spend less time shopping. Once they know what you need, they can suggest investments that fit, the right investments for your specific shopping needs.

How to Shop for a Top-Quality Portfolio

• Fine-tune your financial objectives and make a list of what you think you need. Consult a financial professional for advice or clarification.

• Strike a balance between growth and income investments as determined by your common sense, comfort level, age, and life-style.

• Diversify across different asset classes and industry groups.

• Ladder maturities in bond portfolios so your bonds come due at different times.

• Understand what you own. If you don't understand it, don't own it.

• Review your portfolio at least every three to six months. The Girl Scout motto "Be Prepared!" is applicable to every aspect of your financial life. Anticipate change—divorce, widowhood, unemployment, salary increases and decreases, retirement, and so on. Life happens.

• If any investment is at odds with your objectives or makes you feel uncomfortable, consult your financial adviser. If you don't agree with the advice you get, and still feel strongly about making a change in your portfolio—do it! Trust your instincts.

• The bottom line is that when it comes to creating your portfolio there are a zillion investments out there. But in order for you to meet *your* needs, the choices can be narrowed down tremendously. Only consider what is applicable to *your* financial objectives. Once you know what you need, you can rule out everything else.

Finally, remember the real secret to a good portfolio: Think smart, plan ahead, and don't shop 'til you drop!

ARE STOCKS RISKIER THAN BONDS?

 No! Stocks and bonds come in all different shapes and sizes. A top-quality stock is a lot safer than a low-quality bond. In the late 1980s many investors were financially shell-shocked when their supposedly safe junk bonds headed south big time. Perception doesn't always equal reality when it comes to stocks and bonds.

Secret #6...

Your Safety Net: The Two Cs and Two Ds: Getting Down to Basics

I've always been interested in money. As the older of two daughters, I was my father's son by default. While my sister was in the kitchen with Mom, I was talking money with Dad. He was fascinated by the financial world, and every night we'd sit together, side by side, watching business shows. Our dinner conversations almost always revolved around some aspect of money and finance. People who know me now say that as a young girl I must have resembled Michael J. Fox's Alex P. Keaton character in a skirt.

When I first began my career as a financial consultant, I was totally confident in my ability. And why shouldn't I have been? My background was in finance, and my strong suit had always been money. It never occurred to me that entering this traditionally male-dominated field wasn't the right thing to do until my male colleagues began telling me, "You're never going to do well in this business, Esther. This is not a woman's business."

I have to admit that I started to doubt myself. Suddenly I was in the fifth grade again. This was when my art teacher told me that I couldn't draw. Now I had always thought I drew pretty well, but she didn't think so. And since she was the expert, I trusted her opinion. Do you know, that was the last time I ever drew?

So here I was again in the uncomfortable spot of being told I couldn't do something that I had always done well. And it didn't help that the men I worked with kept calling me "honey"—especially since I wasn't married to any of them. Here I was, eager, ready, and prepared to talk money, and all they wanted to do was pat me on the head.

My frustrations grew. I knew I was beating my head against a closed door. The sign hanging on it might have been invisible, but I read it loud and clear—No Women Allowed. There was no way I could turn myself into a man, but there had to be a way for me to do professionally what I had always loved.

Then that little voice deep within me spoke up: "Come on, Esther. This isn't the fifth grade. You can make this work. *Why not just adapt this business to who you are and what you believe in?*"

I was a woman, money was my business, and I knew and believed that women were as capable as men when it came to handling money. Their only problem was that they didn't have the information. At that moment the light bulb went on. I had my epiphany: The information women needed was at *my* fingertips.

My door opened to an entire community of women, convinced that they couldn't do money and eager to listen to what I had to say. In fact, I usually open my speeches to different women's groups with, "I always enjoy talking to an audience of women because you actually want to hear what I have to say!"

Once I decided to work specifically with women, it was clear that they needed to learn about handling and investing their money in a language that was simultaneously informative, friendly, and familiar. They needed simplicity and directness because most of the financial experts they had consulted with had made everything seem complicated.

For example, I was timidly asked by a woman at one lecture what a zero-coupon bond is. I explained to her that it is a bond that you buy at a discount below $1,000, that pays you no interest along the way (hence the name *zero coupon*). You get paid full par value ($1,000) when the bond matures. She responded, "Do you know how many times I've asked that question? This is the first time I've ever understood the answer!" She was smiling. She was excited. She finally understood an aspect of investing that had obviously confused her for a long time.

"Not knowing" had made her very uncomfortable about money. The knowledge I gave her empowered her to take the next step:

letting go of the fear that "I can't 'do' money" and being receptive to investment information.

The Origins of My Investment Philosophy

In analyzing my investment philosophy and how it could best help other women, I put myself on the other side of the desk. I thought, Esther, what if you hadn't been raised to "do" money? How would you feel? Would you be able to feel comfortable with the task of investing your money if you didn't have the knowledge that men seem automatically to possess? Wouldn't you be afraid to dip your toes in the money waters? What would it take to make you confident enough to get started?

I began thinking about the basics of life that we all need for survival, security, and emotional well-being: we all need common sense, comfort with our decisions, diversification in our lives, and discipline to follow through with our goals and to keep ourselves well informed.

A pattern emerged. These familiar basics for successful living could be easily applied to investing. It seemed logical to use these basics as a framework for my investment philosophy.

Within this framework I created four categories, which I call *the two Cs and two Ds:* common sense, comfort level, diversification, and discipline. Although my two Cs and two Ds investment philosophy isn't 100 percent foolproof (nothing in investing is), it is an excellent starting point. And this philosophy isn't just for the beginning investor. It may be simple to understand and easy to use, but that doesn't mean it's not equally applicable and important for sophisticated investors as well.

When financial and economic climates are unstable, it's wise to go back to the basics—the things that keep us safe and provide sound guidelines. Closely following the two Cs and two Ds means you're sticking with the basics, allowing you to maintain some control over your investments even though the general financial picture may appear out of control.

The First C: Your Common Sense

Your first guideline for investing is nothing more than relying on your common sense. It's extremely simple—but it's not simplistic.

For the first-time investor, *common sense* can help you define your financial objectives and keep you on course as you choose the appropriate asset classes in which to shop. If you're going to need X amount of dollars in three months, your common sense tells you to stay with short-term, risk-free investments. Your common sense will also tell you not to invest in very aggressive financial instruments. This automatically discounts the top tier of the money triangle. You won't shop there because you *can't* shop there—you can't afford to lose money.

Commonsense investing means that you invest in what you understand, that you invest in what you know. Use what your own eyes and ears are showing you and telling you. This means avoiding the "hot tips" you get at the golf course or at a cocktail party.

When you invest because you know the facts, you also invest in things you understand on a personal level. For instance, if you're in the toy business, common sense should tell you to think about investing in your own toy company or even in a competitor's company if they've got a new toy coming to market.

It never fails to amaze me when people who work in one business call me up and want to know about something totally different—and usually it involves something they barely understand.

Let's stay with the toy business analogy: Someone in the toy business will call me up and want to know about investing in biotechnology stocks—which they know absolutely nothing about—when clearly what they know is the toy business.

I have to bring them back to their good sense, their common sense, by asking them, "Think about what your company has coming out for the Christmas selling season. What are your new products? And if your company doesn't have anything great, what are your competitors up to?"

Besides their competitors, I ask them to think about other industries that are related to toy manufacturing or maybe large toy distribution outlets. You can continue thinking like this—I call it "bridging" —as you consider any businesses that are even remotely connected with your own. What's important is that you are staying in friendly territory—in the realm of the familiar.

Again, the basic premise is to invest in what you know, in what makes sense to you. It's when you go too far afield that you get lost. And unless you're awfully lucky, that little trip could cost you a bundle.

If you're a travel agent, think about investing in travel companies, airlines, or other travel-related products. Now do some bridging: What about popular clothing manufacturers that make affordable resort wear? What about luggage companies? What about popular hotels? As you can see, the possibilities are endless. All you need are the facts and some creative thinking, combined with what you're familiar with and what you already know.

Commonsense investing involves your intuition as well. If you are a Nordstrom shopper, like the quality and service that you get there, and usually leave spending double the amount you intended to spend —you should look into buying Nordstrom stock. It's probably an investment that makes sense. Think about it. If you're that impressed by the services provided, chances are other shoppers feel the same way. A company like this will probably make for a good, steady growth investment.

But if the economy is starting to slow down and people are cutting back on their spending, your intuition may tell you to question this investment. If people have less money to spend, common sense tells you that they may start to shop at stores less expensive than Nordstrom. This is not to say that it changes the investment value of Nordstrom—but it could dampen the company's earnings. Rather than invest in Nordstrom at this time, you may want to look into other popular, more moderately priced, department stores. Or you may want to follow Nordstrom's stock for a while and see if it goes down. If it does, and you still like the company, you may want to buy it with the intention of holding on to it until the economy improves. This is a good example of common sense and intuition working together.

You can also use your common sense to invest in *themes* that interest you. For instance, if you believe, as I do, that the demographic trend in this country is clearly skewing older, you should research health care companies, cruise lines, leisure activities, and other industries that benefit from the aging of America.

If you've been reading about events in Europe and the ex–Soviet Union, you're probably aware of how rapidly that part of the world is changing. There is a growing population of consumers in both Western and Eastern Europe and in the Baltic republics eager for American goods and services. Common sense dictates that the beneficiaries of this sudden growth will be companies that have a large volume of sales overseas.

Look at McDonald's. This fast-food chain is all over the world. The day the Berlin Wall came down, McDonald's stock went up. The joke among stock traders was that all the East Germans were rushing to the nearest McDonald's for their first Big Mac!

The same thing happened in Russia. The moment communism was out, McDonald's was in. It's not unheard of for Russians to wait in line for three hours to get Chicken McNuggets and a large order of fries.

And the clothing company Levi Strauss sponsored the first "Best Twins" contest in Moscow, where twins from all over Russia competed for the title of "Best Twins." Of course, the winners in the teenage division received Levi's jeans, Levi's jackets, Levi's everything. Obviously Levi Strauss has made itself known in the new Russia.

Commonsense investing can also involve your *social awareness.* When AIDS was first discussed publicly, most of us preferred to look the other way. It's not pleasant to think about, and I'm sure most of us said, "It can't happen to me." But common sense tells us *(if we listen)* that AIDS is everyone's problem—and a growing one. Investors who invested early on in companies researching potential AIDS cures made a lot of money, particularly after Magic Johnson announced that he had tested HIV positive. The amount of money that has poured into these companies since then is incredible. A tragic situation, but an excellent investment opportunity, especially if you invested in these companies five years ago. Does that sound ghoulish? Well, aside from being an excellent investment opportunity, what about being an excellent opportunity to help fund AIDS research (research that may lead to the discovery of an effective cure)?

One thing to remember about using your common sense in investing is that you don't need a Ph.D. in economics. You don't have to read *The Wall Street Journal* every morning, either—unless you want to. (The business section of your local newspaper can be interesting, too.) But, truly, making a good investment decision often involves nothing more than awareness and personal observation.

My "chicken lady," as I endearingly call her, is one of my sharpest clients. She bases all her investment decisions on her personal observations. A few years ago she was dining out and noticed that everyone was suddenly eating chicken. The menu at her favorite restaurant had even changed, increasing its selection of chicken dishes. This was during the time people were finally waking up to the reality of cholesterol and, concerned about their cholesterol levels, were cutting down on their consumption of red meat.

The following day she called me to find out who was the largest poultry producer in the United States, and then she instructed me to invest heavily. Needless to say, her observations paid off. Butchers have figured out at least a hundred different ways to pluck and prepare a chicken. It was a brilliant investment and based on pure common sense!

My friend Judy, whom I hadn't seen since she moved to Ohio, called me up one day about three years ago to tell me that she had received a nice Christmas bonus. Her problem was that she couldn't decide what to invest in. I asked her what was going on in her life and what her friends were doing.

She told me, "Well, it seems like everybody is having a baby. In fact, Jerry and I are thinking maybe we should have another child."

Since Judy was focusing on having another baby, I suggested that she look into the different companies that manufacture items that babies need and use. I urged her to research "baby stuff," everything from diapers to clothing—things that really made common sense.

A month later Judy called to tell me that she had decided to invest in a company that developed those wonderful front pouches you carry your baby in. They have straps that go over your shoulders and tie in the back. This way parents can hold their baby and still have use of their arms and hands. Now that's common sense!

The Second C: Your Comfort Zone

Your second guideline for investing comes from the mouth of my grandmother who always said, "If it doesn't feel good, don't do it." This is a good philosophy for life and certainly a good philosophy for investing. Listen to your warm fuzzies!

In fact, feeling comfortable with your investments is so important that even if it means missing out on an excellent investment opportunity, *always stay within your comfort zone.*

Your *comfort level* will help you determine your risk tolerance. Certain investments can be winnowed out if they are not consistent with your risk tolerance. This means that if you are interested in very aggressive growth stocks, you have to be prepared to lose money. If you're not, aggressive growth stocks aren't for you, because what goes up also comes down—sometimes with a thud.

In 1991 biotechnology stocks were the hot ticket. Everyone was buying biotech, and that sector went up, up, up! But in early 1992 it fell out of favor. Those who bought at the top lost a great deal of money.

When you use your comfort level as one of your shopping guides, you won't shop 'til you drop because your comfort level dictates what you can and cannot handle. Staying within your comfort level is the easiest way to eliminate unnecessary shopping. And it's actually the most important factor in determining what works for you in your portfolio.

If a client tells me that she is willing to risk losing only 5 percent of her principal, I can winnow out about 90 percent of all the investment alternatives that are available. This is because they are going to be riskier than the client can handle.

When using your common sense and comfort level for investment decisions, age and life-style are also going to be important factors. If an older client is comfortable investing in aggressive, and even speculative, investments, common sense may dictate that she shouldn't, especially if she wants to use money for speculative investments that she truly needs for income investments.

I've had calls from retired clients who are ready to invest a bundle in an "it's going to the moon" penny stock. They're convinced that the top tier of the money triangle is where they're going to hit it big. My job is to reintroduce them to their common sense. They may end up calling *me* an old fuddy-duddy, but at least I've kept them from throwing out money.

On the other hand, a retired client who invests strictly in the first tier of the money triangle is, in effect, growing poor safely. Inflation will decimate her portfolio. She has to listen to her common sense and stretch her comfort level to accommodate some second-tier investing. This may be difficult for her at first, but it's also necessary.

A beginning investor who has just inherited an extensive portfolio may be prepared to take a lot of risk. Not only does her comfort level make her feel that it's okay to do so, but it may in fact make sense if she has a great deal of investment capital and can afford to be moderately aggressive.

On the other hand, a beginning investor with high-risk tolerance may have very little money to invest. Common sense dictates that she should begin with more conservative investments. Ideally there will come a time when her investment capital expands to meet her comfort level.

A lot of financial advisers are very persuasive individuals—they could get you to buy just about anything. But the trick is that regardless of how convincing a financial adviser, best friend, or your rich aunt Harriet might be, don't invest in anything that doesn't feel right to you.

In making investment decisions, I see a major difference between men and women and the choices they make based on their respective comfort levels. Here is where men and women definitely part company. Men claim to have a very analytical approach to money matters, while women take a gut-level, comfort zone approach.

A woman will say, "Sometimes I just don't think it's quite right, and if you ask me to explain why, I can't tell you." Men, on the other hand, like to quantify.

My husband, Leo, a CPA, is always saying, "Explain it to me. Tell me why you don't like this investment." He wants to listen to me spell out in every detail with a zillion reasons why I feel the way I do. I have to tell him that it just doesn't feel right, it makes me uncomfortable. After this "explanation," he just looks at me, totally perplexed, even after nineteen years of marriage.

But my response is valid. Call it comfort zone, call it intuition, call it sixth sense. But it works in the world of money.

One of the most sucessful investors I know is my client Amanda, a top-notch attorney. She is what I call a "seat of the pants" investor. She listens to her gut instincts and operates within her comfort zone. She's a terrifically intuitive investor who values her own judgment and sticks closely to what feels right for her. If it works for her, why not for you?

When using your comfort zone as one of your investment guidelines, you must also evaluate what you perceive as safe. I bring this up because most people perceive stocks as very risky—they consider *all stocks* unsafe investments.

As a financial professional, I strongly believe that you should include a number of top-quality stocks in your portfolio. And for good reason. Historically, stocks have proven to be excellent investments over time. From 1940 to 1990, blue-chip stocks as represented by the S&P 500 returned 11.6 percent. In comparison, "safe" Treasury bills returned only 4.4 percent. Without a doubt, over time stocks have outpaced inflation better than almost any other investment. And over the long term, they have certainly outperformed bonds and CDs.

But in keeping with my investment philosophy, if you don't want to own stocks—if it makes you too nervous and you're losing sleep at night—don't own them. It doesn't matter what I think or what any other financial professional thinks. If you're not comfortable with stocks, don't invest in them.

Now, even though I just said what I said, before you cross stocks off your list of investment possibilities, do some homework and talk to several different financial advisers. You may want to pick a couple of stocks, pretend that you've bought them, and track them for a couple of months to see how well they do. This may help you feel more at ease with stocks, and you may want to consider adding some conservative ones to your portfolio. I wouldn't stress this point if I wasn't convinced that stock ownership can be so profitable.

However, do be careful of the investments that you perceive as safe because they seem safe. Just because an investment is trendy doesn't mean it's good or safe.

For example, in the late 1980s people perceived bonds—all bonds —as being very safe. They invested heavily in junk bonds with the promise of a high yield and a big return. Sadly, many junk bonds were bought by retired, elderly investors as supposedly safe proxies for lower-yielding money markets.

People wrongly assumed that because these junk bonds looked like bonds and acted like bonds, they were every bit as safe as most other bonds. Unfortunately, these junk bonds quacked loudly and many people got hurt financially—especially older people who would never be able to make up these financial losses in their lifetime.

When you invest within your comfort level *and* understand exactly what you're investing in, you can do exceptionally well. Witness the growth of "socially responsible" investing in recent years. As the public becomes increasingly concerned about issues ranging from the environment to those affecting the social fabric of our lives, many investors have begun to screen their investments carefully. Today, for example, there are mutual funds that offer not only excellent growth potential, but also the ability to invest in environmentally friendly companies, companies that provide on-premises day care and those that promote fair hiring practices.

It just goes to show that you can use your common sense, stay within your comfort level, and make a great deal of money by investing in what you believe in.

The First D: Diversification

Diversification is Wall Street–ese for "Don't put all your eggs in one basket." When you diversify, you're taking your comfort level one step farther. The idea is that even though you're comfortable with an investment decision, you don't put every dollar you have into it. Think about it. If you have every dollar of your retirement plan in money markets, CDs, or bonds, you have absolutely no inflation protection.

So where do you begin? You need to structure your portfolio as a money triangle (see diagram on the following page).

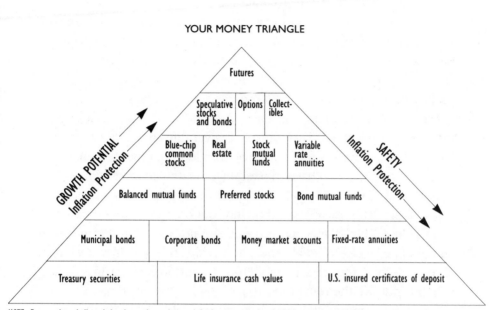

YOUR MONEY TRIANGLE

NOTE: Except where indicated, bonds, stocks, and mutual funds are assumed to be high quality and investment grade.

To stay within your comfort level, create the base or bottom third of your triangle with what I call "sleep at night" investments. These investments are the safest of all and include CDs, money markets, Treasury securities, cash value of life insurance, high-quality corporate and municipal bonds, and fixed-rate annuities. These investments will not make you rich, but they are stable and can provide you with income. They allow you to sleep at night because their value almost never changes.

The middle of your triangle is created by your "inflation fighters" —your growth investments—and should be extremely well diversified. This typically includes a mix of high-quality common and preferred stocks, mutual funds, variable annuities, and high-quality real estate investments.

Precious metals, especially gold, used to be owned as an inflation hedge. Aside from the recent weakness in the precious metals markets in general, I am not convinced that gold is the inflation hedge that it once was and generally don't recommend it as a part of your portfolio.

Finally, at the top of your triangle—if you can afford it and have the stomach for it—are your most aggressive growth investments, including futures contracts, speculative common stocks and bonds, collectibles, and options. This is where you invest only as much money as you can afford to lose. For some clients, especially when it comes to retirement money, this top little triangle remains blank.

So how much should you have in each level of the triangle? Although its application is not universal given life-style differences, the basic rule of thumb is that your age should equal the percentage of your portfolio that you have in fixed-income or safe investments.

If you are forty years old, you should put 40 percent in very safe investments. This means good-quality bonds, CDs, money markets, and the like. The balance, 60 percent, should be invested in inflation fighters like stocks, mutual funds, and real estate. Or, if you want to have some play money and can afford it, put 50 percent in inflation fighters and save the remaining 10 percent for speculation.

Conversely, an investor who is sixty years old would do the opposite, placing 60 percent in very safe investments and 40 percent in the growth investments that are inflation fighters.

The logic in these percentages is simple. Two things come into play: inflation and risk tolerance. A sixty-year-old, in terms of average life expectancy, is going to have fewer years of inflation eroding her principal than the forty-year-old. Also, a sixty-year-old can't afford as much risk because she has less time to recover her losses.

A twentysomething woman, on the other hand, can't afford *not* to take a fair amount of risk. If she plays it too safe, inflation will wreak havoc on her portfolio. A twenty-five-year-old should resist the temptation to be overly conservative, placing no more than 25 percent in very safe investments and 75 percent in growth investments.

You can, of course, adjust these percentages—just remember to apply your common sense and stay within your comfort zone. But it is critical that you do diversify.

Diversification may call for more shopping instead of less. If you're creating a first-time portfolio or making changes in an existing portfolio (or one that you've acquired through divorce or an inheritance), you will need to do a fair amount of shopping to achieve diversification across the different asset classes. This may encompass a wide range of investments, but even so, I can help you narrow down your choices.

How? Because when you diversify your portfolio, you are still going to use your common sense and stay within your comfort level. This will automatically winnow out certain cash equivalents, stocks, bonds, and mutual funds.

A good example is my client Barbara, who just turned sixty and is thinking about taking early retirement. She's been with her company for over thirty years and has a well-funded 401(k) to draw on. Barbara will still need some additional income, and she doesn't have much risk tolerance. That information alone certainly winnows out aggressive growth stocks, options, and commodities. She already owns a fair amount of real estate, so that's out, too. And she has no interest in precious metals, so these get eliminated as well. By the time we actually get to diversification, the shopping list of investment possibilities has already been pared down considerably by applying Barbara's common sense and comfort level.

Barbara's starting point is her real estate and her 401(k), of which half is invested in growth stocks and half is invested in a money market. To this we add Treasuries with staggered maturities of three, five, seven, and ten years. She also decides to invest in a basket of utility stocks for dividends and some potential for growth. Now she's diversified with growth stocks, income stocks, bonds, real estate, and a money market without having to shop 'til she drops!

The Second D: Discipline

As far as I'm concerned, of the two Cs and two Ds, discipline is the real key to successful investing. Let's return to my earlier example of the hot tip you get on the golf course or at a cocktail party. Investing in one of these so-called hot tips is not investing—it's what I call playing. Playing can be fun, but it belongs at the very top of your money triangle because it is so risky. It's not investing—it's gambling.

Discipline is what I always say separates the girls from the women.

It means not talking about biotech stocks if you need income. It means no window-shopping—unless you have extra play money. It allows your common sense and comfort level to keep you on course. And it means revisiting your objectives and sticking to them . . . not chasing some long shot that can either hit the moon or crash and burn. Your discipline keeps you from wandering into the evening wear department when you have only enough money for one new outfit for work.

Discipline means making a financial plan and sticking to it. It means creating a plan that you intend to follow.

When a client comes to my office for the first time, I always ask, "What do you want your money to do for you?"

The typical response is, "Well, I want it to grow."

To which I respond, "Okay, that works. But define this for me. Let's narrow it down a little bit. Does this mean you want a 10 percent return per year? Does this mean that you want to outpace inflation by 5 percent? Does this mean you want X dollars to retire on when you are sixty-five years old?"

Quantifying exactly what you want requires discipline. And it means taking time to think it through and formulate a plan. It's very disturbing to me that most people will spend more time researching and shopping for a new car than they will spend analyzing their retirement needs.

My point is that a large part of the discipline of investing is in knowing what you're investing in—before you actually own it! Find out what's in those pension plan boxes before you check them. Don't assume that if something sounds good, it is. And ask lots of questions until you are absolutely clear about what you're investing in.

Another part of investment discipline is learning to take losses. This is critical, and nobody likes it. In fact, the famous last words of investing are "I'm just waiting to break even!"

For example, you own a stock that cost you $10 a share. Now it's down to $7 a share. This is a substantial loss, 30 percent. Unfortunately, people rarely consider selling at this loss. They wait to break even. Now it's down to $5 a share, which is a 50 percent loss. What percentage do you need to break even? You need a 100 percent gain. Is it likely that this investment will double? That's what you need to break even.

Discipline means taking a loss while it's bearable. It means never getting married to an investment—because we all make mistakes. If we didn't, we'd retire to Tahiti and spend our days sipping mai-tais.

My colleagues and I go to work every morning. Our job is to help you invest. But none of us has all the answers. Common sense tells us this.

If you want to be a successful investor, you must accept that investing is an extremely inexact science. Investments that make sense don't always work out. This is why using your common sense is great at the beginning and why you must use your discipline from beginning to end. And this is why you diversify—because sometimes really good ideas just don't work out. Some do; others don't. There are lots of external variables that affect the markets that none of us can control.

When the 1991 Persian Gulf War broke out, the stock market dropped immediately. Suddenly even high-quality, conservative stocks and mutual funds were down. It reminded me of how humbling an experience investing can be. Just when you think you have it all figured out, a monkey wrench gets thrown in. Suddenly what seemed so right is no longer working out.

This is why, when all else fails, you must go back to the basics. Although nothing can absolutely guarantee investment success, my two Cs and two Ds provide sound guidelines to preserving your wealth.

WHY SHOULD YOU THINK OF "BANKING" AT A BROKERAGE FIRM RATHER THAN AT A BANK?

$Years ago banks were banks and brokerages were brokerages, but today you can do almost all your banking business at a brokerage firm. You can open a checking account and get a credit card— even a gold card—at brokerage firms. Most brokerages can provide notary public services. And if you have securities that you can pledge as collateral, you can borrow money from a brokerage firm. In fact, some brokerages even provide home equity loans.

Secret#7 ...
Your "A Team":
Picking Professional Help

A couple of years ago we renovated our home, which for me became a nightmare that I thought would never end. At one point the general contractor was calling me up every hour and asking me to choose between drywall and plaster and tile and marble and other things I didn't even know existed. I found myself wanting to crawl into bed and hide.

But then I got smart and asked the contractor, "Can you explain what you're talking about? And slowly. I don't understand."

The contractor looked at me as if I had part of my brain missing. He couldn't figure out what the big deal was because this was what he did every day of his life.

I don't know about you, but understanding the difference between drywall and plaster is not the magnum opus of my life. However, when I'm asked to make decisions about something I know nothing about, I get frightened. And I hang out my mental Do Not Disturb sign. Unfortunately, this didn't do much for getting the house finished.

How did I solve this dilemma? By hiring a very professional and patient interior design architect to help me and guide me. She knew everything about everything and was the perfect teacher. She corrected my misperceptions and allowed me to make my own choices as I began to understand more about construction. And as I gained confidence with her guidance, I became more competent.

The way she helped me is the way the right financial advisers can help you. They should guide you, correct any misperceptions you have, and allow you to make your own choices as you learn. Always remember that it's your money, and your investment choices are your decision—good financial advisers will reinforce this. And as you learn more about your finances and become confident that you can manage them, you'll become more competent.

The financial advisers a woman chooses to work with, whether it's only one person or several, are what I call her "A team." These are the people she talks to when she's uncertain about the return on a municipal bond or when she comes across a new investment term that she doesn't fully understand. They answer tax questions and clarify the details of her retirement plan.

As different members of her "A team" help her with her financial planning, depending on their area of expertise, they are patient and professional, people she can relate to. They are people who do not make her feel small or stupid because she doesn't understand something.

Many women who come to see me have been working with financial advisers they don't like. Although they tell me these advisers make them feel uncomfortable, they automatically assume that it's their own fault that they feel this way.

My client Gail can't understand a word her CPA is saying, yet she won't leave him because she has worked with him for years. Gail blames herself for her discomfort with this man—chalking it up to his brilliance and her "stupidity" about money. Besides the lack of self-esteem she feels when it comes to handling her personal finances, there are also emotional issues that keep her tied to this business relationship that doesn't work for her.

"Oh, it's not his fault that I can't understand a word he's saying," explains Gail. "The family joke has always been that I need a seeing-eye dog to find my checkbook! They're right—no wonder I just freeze when my CPA starts rambling off all of those numbers . . . it's overwhelming. But I've been with him for so many years—I know if I leave him, it will really hurt his feelings. I just can't do it."

I have clients who have wills or trusts drawn up and later tell me they had no idea what their attorneys were talking about. They come to me for an explanation. And although I am happy to help, it troubles me that another professional isn't doing his job properly. I always ask my clients, "Don't you think that part of your attorney's job is to explain this to you in a way that you understand? Do you think your attorney is really doing right by you if you're leaving his office totally confused?"

If either of these scenarios sounds familiar to you, I suggest that you reevaluate who's working for you and your money. It is their responsibility to make sure that you understand. This is their area of expertise, not yours. If they can't make it comprehensible, what good are they to you?

You may also want to consider working with female financial advisers instead of male ones. I know this sounds like reverse sexism—but women do know women. A lot of women with whom I work have told me that they communicate better and just feel more comfortable with female professionals. If a problem comes up, they hesitate to say anything to a male adviser. Like Gail, they don't know how to exercise their authority or confront the issue when something doesn't seem right. I think much of this has to do with the fact that there are still so many unresolved issues about money, power, and control between men and women.

If you are seeking financial guidance for the first time, know that *anyone* who makes you feel uncomfortable in any way, *male or female,* is probably not the right adviser for you. Your level of discomfort has nothing to do with your intelligence or your abilities. This adviser may be some unscrupulous person trying to take advantage of you, or he may just be a poor communicator. Either way, keep looking until you feel confident that the person you've chosen is right for you!

Whom You Need and Why You Need Them

So where do you begin? First, try to assess your needs—and be realistic. If you've just finished college and are beginning your career, your financial planning needs will probably be minimal—unless you have a trust fund that needs managing or you have suddenly inherited a large sum of money. Otherwise, all you'll need at this time is someone to help you with your taxes and someone to give you some insight into beginning a financial plan.

Perhaps you're fortysomething and concerned about how much

money you'll need to live comfortably when you retire. Or maybe you're already there, and you want to make the most of your retirement money. Should you leave your growth investments alone or consider shifting them into more income-producing investments? In both situations, more extensive financial planning will be necessary.

Assessing your needs is best done by sitting down with a legal pad and making a list. It's really that easy to get started. On this list might be areas of your financial life that you don't understand as well as any areas that you think are weak. Maybe you have a question about one of the terms I've discussed and you need clarification before you make an investment. Perhaps you're concerned about your ability to budget, your savings habits, or how you're going to plan for your children's college education.

My rule of thumb is that the level of service you need from your financial advisers should be equal to the level of complexity of your finances, your life-style, and your investment portfolio.

If you stick with this rule, you should be able to find appropriate advisers who can provide you with the services that you need without spending a fortune. But *don't* cheap out on financial advice that you really do need. It's worth the money to get your financial house in order. There are places to save money and places to spend money— your "A team" is definitely not the place to scrimp.

There are some people whose lives are in a real financial pickle. They've got tax troubles with the IRS, a messy divorce has left them in financial chaos, or they've aquired a portfolio of stocks and bonds that they don't understand—the list could go on and on. If any of this sounds familiar, or you simply feel that you are in over your head, expect to pay for the financial services that will get you back on track. The money will be well spent—and you'll definitely sleep better at night.

On the other hand, be sensible. It doesn't make sense to spend a lot of money on an extensive financial plan if you really don't need one. This is why it's so important for you to assess your needs to the best of your ability before interviewing potential advisers.

What follows is an overview of the different types of financial advisers and the services they can provide you. Remember, your goal is to build a sound "A team" that supports you, is of service to you, helps you plan and implement your investment decisions, and makes you feel comfortable and financially competent.

CERTIFIED PUBLIC ACCOUNTANT (CPA)

A CPA has passed a national examination, has completed a certain level of financial and accounting education, and must comply with continuing education requirements as well. You'll probably need a CPA to do your tax return—unless your return is very simple.

It's extremely difficult for most people to prepare their own tax returns. Tax reform, which was supposed to simplify everything, has, ironically, made figuring your taxes much more complicated.

I tell my clients that it's not wise for them to tackle their taxes on their own to save money. There are just too many things you have to be aware of, and the tax laws are changing constantly. For instance, if you have a profit-sharing plan, there are specific reporting requirements with which you must comply. If not, the penalties from the IRS could far exceed what you would pay a CPA to do it right. The bottom line is that when you mess up with the IRS there are penalties, late charges, and back interest that you'll have to pay.

Most CPAs aren't professional money managers. But they can help you evaluate the performance of your investment portfolio. They can also help you if you're thinking of buying a business or expanding or streamlining the one you have. Remember, CPAs are trained to crunch numbers—and they can easily do a profit-and-loss analysis for you.

TAX PREPARER

If you are convinced you don't need a CPA to help you with your taxes, consider using a tax preparer. This person is not certified as a CPA is but should be well versed in tax matters. It's a good idea to check around for referrals since tax preparers don't have the same educational background or experience as CPAs.

TAX ATTORNEY

I think tax attorneys are overkill for most people unless you have a specific problem with the IRS or a lawsuit pending. You really don't need to consult a tax attorney unless another financial adviser tells you that you need to. Typically, your CPA will be the first one to tell you if you do need a tax attorney, and she should be able to refer you to a good one.

Most CPAs, tax preparers, and tax attorneys will charge you by the hour for the work they do. CPAs and tax attorneys may require a monthly or onetime retainer—a substantial sum of money up front—that will be applied against hourly fees. Once your billable hours exceed your retainer, you will be billed on an hourly basis.

Some CPAs establish a minimum charge for tax return preparation, regardless of how simple or not so simple your return is. If a CPA's minimum charge is more than your return warrants, ask for a referral to a tax preparer or another CPA who can do a good job for a lower fee.

A good financial adviser is someone who can say, "Frankly, you don't need me. But I can refer you to someone who is quite capable of meeting your needs and will cost you less." Most good financial professionals are not looking to take your money. If you're dealing with ethical people, they won't get you into something you don't need. They'll tell you what they think you really do need and then advise you to use your own judgment.

CERTIFIED FINANCIAL PLANNER (CFP)

To become a licensed CFP you have to pass certificate examinations in six different areas: the financial planning process, risk management, investments, tax planning and management, retirement and employee benefits, and estate planning.

Whether you need help just structuring your budget, or you need something more extensive that might include retirement planning, buying a business, or formulating a long-term investment strategy, talking with a CFP is a good starting point.

Fee-based CFPs charge on an hourly basis. Since they are not selling anything (unlike commission-based or fee-plus-commission-based CFPs), there is no conflict of interest. You're paying by the hour for as much of their time as you need. They can answer specific financial questions as well as help you get an overview of your financial picture.

On a more extensive level, a CFP should have the expertise to prepare a comprehensive financial plan for you. This plan may be done on a *flat fee basis,* meaning that you will be charged a onetime cost for the plan. The plan can encompass areas of your financial life ranging from insurance to investments to pension plans to estate planning. A lot of what CFPs can do depends on their level of expertise and your level of need.

If you're just starting out, you probably don't need a very extensive financial plan. A handwritten one may even do. If your plan is more complicated, it means that more time and energy will have to go into it—and obviously your fee will be higher.

STOCKBROKER

Traditionally stockbrokers are people who buy and sell stocks and bonds. Stockbrokers can also deal with many other financial instruments ranging from CDs to money markets, gold bullion to Japanese yen, or just about any other marketable security. They have to pass a number of different state and national licensing exams to become licensed brokers. Theoretically they have to be knowledgeable about all aspects of the financial marketplace—although this may not always be the case. Some stockbrokers are also insurance-licensed and can advise you about life insurance and fixed and variable annuities. But to do this they must have separate insurance licenses.

Most brokers are commission-based, which means they are paid a percentage of the money you invest when you buy a security and a percentage of the money you receive when you sell a security. It's important to know that brokers charge different percentages for different investments. Their commissions also vary according to the number of dollars being invested.

Usually, when you're investing a larger amount of money, the percentage commission you pay will be smaller. Let's assume that you want to buy one hundred shares of a $50 stock. This may cost you about 2 percent commission. Let's assume you're buying one thousand shares of the same $50 stock. This would cost you a lot less proportionately—only 1.29 percent commission.

There are also different commission structures for different types of investments. For instance, it may cost you more to buy a mutual fund than to buy a zero-coupon Treasury.

WHEN CFPS ACT AS BROKERS
AND WHEN BROKERS ARE ALSO CFPS

Some CFPs, who used to charge on an hourly basis only, now manage their clients' assets using mutual funds, stocks, and bonds. They typically charge a percentage of the assets they manage either instead of, or in addition to, their hourly fees.

In the past, brokers were paid by commission only. Now, since brokers also offer professional money management services, you can opt to pay a flat fee—not commission. This confuses many people because it used to be standard that CFPs were paid by the hour and brokers were paid by commission. Now there is so much overlap between the two that many women don't know which way to turn.

A client, Sharon, called me because she was confused about what I could do for her professionally. Because of my affiliation with PaineWebber, she assumed I was a traditional stockbroker.

Sharon and her husband, both lawyers, needed help with their retirement planning. What confused her was that she knew a lot of stockbrokers, but that wasn't what she needed at the moment. Sharon told me, "I know that you're with a brokerage firm, but you don't strike me as a traditional-type stockbroker. I don't want to buy stocks."

Sharon's confusion is common. People equate the word *broker* with buying stocks, which to them means being aggressive and taking chances. I have to go to great lengths to explain that buying and selling stocks is only a small part of what I do.

I have many clients who don't own even one stock; that's as it should be, because it's not right for them. This is a much different approach from that of some brokers who specialize in buying and selling stocks.

When I meet a new client I tell her, "My job is to understand your overall financial needs. I deal with your CDs, your money market accounts, your mutual funds, your retirement plan, your estate liquidity needs, your tax planning . . . your entire financial picture."

I am both a licensed broker and a CFP, which is why I take a financial-planning approach with my clients. I believe strongly in dealing with the "whole" client. I don't work with just a part of their portfolio. I work with their entire portfolio, in the same way that your doctor examines your whole body, not just your left side.

Very early in my career I knew that I didn't want to be a stock trader. I wanted to deal with my clients' overall financial lives, beginning with investments but also helping with everything from estate planning to insurance needs. Being a broker and a CFP has helped me develop and maintain a sound investment philosophy that is both "wholistic" and long term.

When do you need only a stockbroker? If you want to trade securities actively in the traditional sense. But don't expect a stock trader to be able to answer your tax questions or to deal with your insurance needs—or most other aspects of your financial life. Expect from him only what he is trained to do: buy and sell securities for you.

When do you need only a CFP? If you have no interest in investing at all, but you want help with budgeting, tax planning, or general financial information.

When do you need both? When you want someone involved in *all* aspects of your financial life. This includes trading securities or *not* trading securities if it's not right for you, as well as creating an investment plan that will include constant monitoring of your portfolio.

REGISTERED INVESTMENT ADVISER OR MONEY MANAGER

Registered investment advisers are also known as money managers and rarely deal with anyone who has less than $100,000 to invest. To many of you, I'm sure this sounds like a lot of money. But those of you who have been working for at least twenty years may have that much or more in your pension investments. There's a good chance that your retirement plan is worth a lot more than you think.

A money manager charges a flat fee equal to a percentage of your managed assets. Let's say your money manager charges a 1 percent advisory or management fee. If your portfolio is worth $100,000, your money manager would get 1 percent of that per year—$1,000. If the following year your portfolio is worth $110,000, then your money manager would get 1 percent of that—$1,100. You can see how it's to his benefit to make your portfolio grow. It makes you money and it makes him money.

When your money manager buys and sells stocks and bonds for you, these trades will be done through a broker. This means that you will also have to pay commissions on any transactions in your portfolio.

What's particularly interesting about money managers is that they have discretion over your account—which means they make the buy/sell decisions for you. *But*—and this is an important *but*—you can stipulate in advance what your financial goals are and in what types of securities you're willing to invest. You also have the authority to tell your money manager which brokerage firm and broker to execute trades through.

For example, you might give your money manager $150,000 and tell him that you want only blue-chip stocks and Treasury bills. You might specify that you don't want any of your money invested in companies that manufacture tobacco or liquor products. You might also want at least 35 percent of your portfolio in bonds and the rest of the money invested in growth stocks. And you want him to work with Susan Stockbroker at brokerage firm ABC.

If you don't specify whom you want him to work with, your money manager will place your trades with whomever he chooses. Sometimes he'll work with a specific broker as a "thank you" because that broker has referred business to him. This is not to say that this broker isn't qualified. But by instructing him to work with the broker of your choice, you get an extra player on your "A team" and it doesn't cost you a dime.

By making these decisions, you are managing your money *and* your money manager because you're creating the framework for your investments. It is within this framework that your money manager can then exercise his expertise.

Many women hesitate to take advantage of the control they have over their money manager. It's almost as though they're afraid of stepping on toes. And because much of this is new territory for women, they don't even know that they have these rights. Many women also feel that if they are trusting this money manager to handle their money, they should trust this person's judgment in all things.

If your money manager is reluctant to honor your wishes, he or she may not be the right one for you. Remember that we're talking about *your money and your rights.*

STOCKBROKERS, CFPS, MONEY MANAGERS, AND WRAP FEE ACCOUNTS

Within the world of financial advisers there is a great deal of overlap, and the boundaries separating who does what are often blurred. Recently, broker/dealers and some CFPs began offering a complete investment/management account if you have $100,000 plus to invest. This service is called a "wrap fee." What this means is rather than paying 1 percent to a money manager plus commission fees on any buy/sell transactions, you pay an all-inclusive wrap fee. This fee is usually between 2.5 and 3 percent. The services you get include

- a search service for the appropriate money manager

- the money manager's advisory/management fee

- all commissions on buy/sell transactions

- an ongoing portfolio monitoring service: quarterly performance reports track how well your money manager has done compared with other money managers as well as with industry benchmarks like the S&P 500

I think the big plus in having a wrap fee account is that it allows you to have access to some of the best money managers in the country, who normally have account minimums of $2 million, $5 million, and up. These same people manage vast sums of money for very large corporations, institutions, and pension funds. Through wrap fee arrangements with brokerage firms, individual investors can also benefit from these managers' experience and expertise.

With So Many Choices, How Do You Decide?

With all of these choices, what is the best way for you to proceed? First you need to figure out the dollars involved. For instance, if you have a money manager who trades actively, your commission costs can really add up. But if your money manager has more of a buy and hold philosophy, it may be better just to pay his or her percentage fee plus additional commission costs.

Typically, the more money being managed, the smaller the percentage you should be charged.

Also, the fee to manage a bond (fixed-income) portfolio is generally lower than the fee to manage a stock (equity) portfolio.

Banks versus Brokerages

Years ago, banks were banks and brokerages were brokerages, but today you can do almost all your banking business at a brokerage firm. You can open a checking account and get a credit card—even a gold card—at brokerage firms. Some firms will even return your canceled checks to you each month. Most brokerages can provide notary public services. And if you have securities that you can pledge as collateral, you can even borrow money from a brokerage firm. In fact, some brokerages provide home equity loans.

Why should you think of "banking" at a brokerage firm rather than at a bank? First, because the safety level of a brokerage can be greater than a bank's. Brokerages are required to carry $500,000 SIPC (Securities Investor Protection Corporation) insurance for each account. Some brokerage accounts carry up to $25 million of insurance.

If you perceive greater safety in a brokerage—and in some cases it's not just perception, it's reality—you may want to consider shifting your money market and even your checking account to a brokerage firm. Also, consider the interest rate on your bank checking, money market, or savings account. Often brokerages will pay higher interest rates. They also may offer both federal and state tax-free money market accounts.

Although it certainly makes sense to consider "banking" at brokerages, I do advise clients to keep either a checking or savings account at a bank so that they have access to a safety-deposit box for important papers, jewelry, and so on. Brokerages also don't provide traveler's checks, which is an important service that banks provide.

If you think a brokerage firm can do as well as (or better than) your bank, think seriously about making a switch. The more you consolidate the better, because it makes it much easier to keep track of what you have and where it's invested.

A good example of the need to consolidate involves a new client, Rita, who called me because she was about to undergo life-threatening surgery. Her attorney had advised Rita to consolidate all her accounts under the name of her family trust to avoid probate in case she died, and he had referred her to me for help.

Rita was dealing with twelve different banks. This meant that she had to run all over town two days before her surgery, signing authorization papers to move her accounts to her new trust account at my firm. Had Rita consolidated her accounts years earlier, she could have been relaxing before the surgery, which is what she needed to do.

But just as you shouldn't keep your money in twelve different places, don't keep every penny you have in one place, either. Shop around and make comparisons, asking different banks and brokerages, "What can you do for me?"

This is a hard question for many women to ask because they have spent a good portion of their lives asking others, "What can I do for you?"

Where Do You Begin?

Now that you understand what different financial advisers and institutions can do for you, it's time to begin looking. Getting referrals from friends and business associates is an excellent starting point.

Don't let your fingers do the walking through the Yellow Pages. To me, that's like flying blind.

The professional people in my life, whether dentists, doctors, or attorneys, have all been referrals. I want someone I trust to tell me, "I went to this person, and here's the story . . . here's how he [or she] helped me."

When one of my children needed braces, I asked my dentist who his kids' orthodontist was. When it comes to dental care, he knows who's who. It makes sense that he would be able to judge an orthodontist with a more professional eye than I could. It made sense to me to talk to the person he recommended.

If you're looking for a CPA, it makes sense to ask your banker and your broker who prepares their tax returns. If you need a broker, ask your CPA who handles her investments. Financial advisers you already have should be able to refer you to other advisers you still need.

Before you meet with anyone, make some preliminary telephone calls. Investigate all your options and don't disregard any potential resource. And when you make your calls, *don't ask anyone, "What do you do?"*

A better question is, "Are you the appropriate person for me to speak to? Here's what I need. . . . If you're not the right person, whom do you suggest I talk to?"

This framework for your questions shows you to be knowledgeable and puts the other person at attention because you know exactly what you need. This is empowering, making you feel that you're really taking control of your financial life.

Most women have problems just asking these questions, because this is new territory for many of them and they're afraid they'll sound stupid. I always say to my clients, "How are you ever going to learn, or know what you need to know, unless you ask?"

Picking and Choosing

Never forget that you're in control because it's your money. And whoever you choose to be part of your "A team" is going to have to meet your standards. Yes, *your* standards. Here are the ten most important questions you should ask potential "A team" members when you interview them:

1. Tell me about your firm. How long have you been in business? Do you have a minimum account size or a minimum fee?

2. What is your professional background? Why are you qualified to advise me? What's your track record?

3. Can you describe your typical client? (The answer should include age, average income, and makeup of mostly men or mostly women.)

4. What is your investment philosophy? Would you say that you are conservative, aggressive, or middle of the road in your approach to money? What types of investments do you personally own? (It's important that your adviser's philosophy match your own. If not, you need to know this going in because you will probably have conflicts at some point in working with this person.)

5. How do you feel about a woman's ability to manage money? Who handles the money in your own family?

6. Do your clients rely solely on you for advice, or do they do a lot of their own homework? How much guidance do you give your clients? Do you encourage them to take the initiative? Also, if I don't understand what you're talking about, are you willing to explain it until I do?

7. How often do you speak to your clients? On a regular basis or only when specific needs arise? Who will actually handle my account and take my questions when I call?

8. How do you like to interact with your clients' other professional advisers? Do you think you work easily with other members of their team?

9. What sets you apart from others in your field? What makes you different or special?

10. Why do you want to do business with me? What do you expect from me? What can I expect from you?

And here are the ten most important questions potential "A team" advisers should ask you:

1. Tell me about yourself. Who are you—personally and professionally?

2. Have you always made money decisions, or is this a new experience for you? How do you feel about being here?

3. What has been your best money experience, and what has been your worst?

4. Who are your other advisers? Are you comfortable with them? Are they meeting your needs?

5. What is your income? How much do you owe? Do you expect an inheritance, promotion, or anything else that will suddenly affect your financial picture?

6. What are your savings patterns? Do you have a retirement plan, college education fund, life insurance?

7. What do you own now? CDs, money markets, mutual funds, stocks, other investment vehicles? Do you want to make changes? Why?

8. How comfortable are you with taking risks? What do you consider risky?

9. What are your financial goals? Please quantify, beyond "making money." What are your reasons for investing?

10. What else do I need to know about you to help you in the best way I can?

During the interview, listen to your own feelings. Do you really like this person? I think you should work only with people you like and with whom you feel comfortable.

Body language is important. A real professional will talk to you directly, make eye contact, but in no way be suggestive or patronizing. Someone who starts calling you "sweetheart" either has a hidden agenda or doesn't really respect you.

Also, make sure you check out the "trappings." Is the office over-done? Underdone? Is the adviser's desk heaped with disorganized papers—or does he or she seem to have everything under control with easy access to information? And how do they treat the people who work for them? If they're rude to their employees, chances are eventually they'll be rude to you, too.

Finally, beware of bulldozing! Stay away from people who try to make you feel inept, foretelling a future of gloom, doom, and destitution if you don't do business with them. And don't let anyone boss you around.

Remember, the people you hire work for you, not the other way around.

Scheduling Your First Working Appointment

Before you see any financial adviser for your first working appointment, there are several questions you should ask when you call to schedule your time:

"What information do you need from me to help you do your job?"

"What are some of the questions you'll have that I can prepare the answers to in advance so our time will be well spent?"

"What documents or paperwork do you need me to bring?"

When clients come to me for our first meeting, I like to see copies of their tax returns and statements from their banks and brokerages so that I can evaluate their portfolios properly. Having this information allows me to work more efficiently and gives me a better sense of who my client is.

Prepare as much as you can in advance and leave what you don't understand, what is beyond your scope, to your "A team." This means organizing receipts, account numbers and records, and any other pertinent information about your finances. By doing the footwork, not only do you save time and money, but you'll have a better understanding of the questions you need to ask. For example, if you sit down and do a six-month analysis of your checkbook, you can see where your money is coming from and where it's going. This may lead you to some specific questions for your financial adviser:

"I've been spending too much money. How can I cut back?"

"I don't seem to have anything planned for retirement. Can you assist me in this direction?"

"How much of my savings should go into short-term investments? How much should be longer term?"

If you don't come to the first appointment prepared, you may feel overwhelmed. You'll end up wasting a lot of time trying to answer questions that you're not ready for.

Paying your financial adviser to do the preparatory work for you is fine, but understand that you're paying for this convenience. It's like paying a moving company to do everything, when you could have packed and marked the boxes yourself. It's your choice, but a more costly one.

Some Tips for Working Successfully with Your "A Team"

• Don't be patronized. Don't let anyone be oversolicitious or condescending. And don't let anyone call you "honey" unless that happens to be your first name.

• Don't be overwhelmed by bankerspeak or brokerese. Ask for an English translation of any financial jargon you don't understand.

• Don't rush. Take your time deciding with whom to do business. Interview at least two CPAs, two brokers, and two bankers. It takes time, but it's worth it.

• Don't ever let anyone make you feel incompetent. Lack of experience should never be confused with lack of intelligence. Seek out professionals who will educate and guide you in a professional and caring way.

• Don't stay with a financial professional you're not satisfied with. If you choose an inappropriate person the first time, learn from the experience and try again. Mistakes don't last forever.

• Do ask questions. What is the person's professional background? Investment philosophy? Approach to financial planning? Level and depth of expertise?

• Do value rapport and personal compatibility. Do you like this person and feel good about building a long-term professional relationship?

• Do pay attention to body language, speech patterns, and appearance. Look for professionals who are competent, confident, and caring. People who take pride in themselves take pride in their work.

• Do ask for referrals, but not from someone who calls you cold or someone you don't know. Their "referrals" may be as suspect as the services or investments they are peddling.

• Do trust your instincts. Listen to that inner voice that instinctively guides you. Facts, statistics, and performance records are all critically important—but so is your intuition. Trust it and use it!

And regardless of what's happening in your personal life, do recognize that your "A team" is a central part of your financial life. When it comes to your economic well-being, creating and maintaining your "A team" is important—critically important. Think of your "A team" as the foundation that is going to support your financial house of wealth.

PART THREE

Financial Strategies: Where It All Comes Together

SHOULD I BE WATCHING MY STOCKS EVERY DAY?

 Only if you're a trader hoping to make a quick killing. Serious investors are in for the long term. They buy quality and stay tuned. If you like to follow your stocks closely, that's fine. Just don't let the day-to-day vagaries of the stock market derail your investment plan.

Secret #8 . . .

If the Shoes Don't Fit, Don't Shorten Your Feet: Deciding on an Investment Strategy

---

A husband and wife, both clients of mine, heard the same stock tip at a cocktail party. The following day each called within twenty minutes of the other and asked me to purchase the stock. They maintain separate accounts and invest independently of one another.

Several weeks later the "cocktail party" stock took a nosedive. How did they respond?

The husband called me and said, "That stock turned out to be a dog. I want to sell!" For him, the decision to sell was as easy as casting aside an old pair of shoes that no longer fit him so he could slip into a pair of brand-new ones.

His wife called later in the day. "Can you believe how stupid I was to buy this stock? I want to hold on until I break even," she said.

This little scenario is an excellent example of how the emotional dynamics of men and women differ when they invest. Men externalize investment decisions. When an investment does poorly, they are quick to blame the investment and cut their losses. They are eager to move on to another investment.

But women internalize investment decisions. Often they chastise themselves, lament their inability to choose wisely, and label themselves "stupid" when an investment goes south. I repeatedly have to remind women to step away from the emotional issues that can affect their money decisions.

Separating Your Emotions from Your Money

Unfortunately, women investors have a difficult time separating their hearts from their pocketbooks.

For them, getting emotionally bent out of shape when an investment fails is just the tip of the iceberg. I've seen them really go through the emotional wringer when it comes to financial dealings with male friends, family members, and especially husbands-to-be.

Prenuptial agreements are the perfect example. Most wealthy men insist on them; most wealthy women don't. Their emotions take over. They are afraid of rocking the boat. The last thing a woman wants to do is alienate her future husband by demanding a prenuptial agreement. Her great fear is that if he objects and she insists, he'll walk away and the marriage will end before it ever begins.

It's interesting to me that wealthy men rarely have this problem. As far as they're concerned, a prenuptial agreement is strictly a business decision. They have money to protect. It's got nothing to do with love. And their wives-to-be don't hesitate to sign on the dotted line because they want the marriage. They may have their doubts—but they are determined to squeeze their feet into those glass slippers, no matter how tight the fit!

When I have a client who is about to marry, and she is bringing into the marriage substantial investments and money that she's earned on her own, I do my best to enlighten her about the financial realities should the marriage end. It is certainly not what every bride-to-be wants to think about: her marriage ending before she's even had a chance to say "I do."

But my point is that if you enter a marriage with substantial assets and no prenuptial agreement, lots of dollars may walk right out the door along with your ex-husband should the marriage ultimately end.

If you know this going in, and you're comfortable with your decision, fine. Some women tell me that they understand the possible consequences should their marriage end. And although they may not like it, as my client Marjorie said: "That's just the way it has to be." That's not necessarily so, as I told Marjorie. But, sadly, I've met very few women who take care of themselves and their money when it comes to prenups.

This may be the one time in a woman's financial life when her comfort level and her common sense are truly at odds.

If you're about to marry, having a prenuptial agreement is a decision that only you can make, but I suggest you think about it on all levels before ruling it out. Play out the potential scenarios should you and your husband commingle your assets and eventually split up. You could potentially lose half of everything you've worked so hard to achieve. Could you still afford to maintain your life-style, drive the same car, buy your favorite clothes, take weekend trips, even buy a pair of shoes when the old ones no longer fit?

If you're already married and don't have a prenuptial agreement, you may still be able to protect your assets with a postnuptial agreement. It basically serves the same purpose as a prenuptial agreement —it just happens after the fact.

When Ruth received a large inheritance from her grandmother, she used the money for the down payment on the home she and her husband, Steve, had dreamed of owning someday. Steve didn't contribute a penny. The house was titled jointly, which meant that if their marriage ended, he could potentially get half of the house.

Fortunately Steve agreed to a postnuptial agreement, and together they went to a family law attorney. The three of them went over the records, and after reviewing who paid what on the mortgage, property taxes, and the down payment, it was determined that should their marriage end, 85 percent of the house would belong to Ruth and 15 percent would belong to Steve.

Postnuptials can also include other provisions. If you didn't discover until after the wedding that your husband tends to overspend with credit cards, consider this: I know a woman who thought she would be receiving a hefty divorce settlement and was shocked to find out that she was responsible for half of the credit card debt her husband had racked up—debt that she didn't even know about! Had she known during the marriage what she found out later, she could have drafted a postnup stipulating which credit cards were her husband's—and were his sole financial responsibility.

Whether it involves a prenuptial or a postnuptial agreement, wealthy men don't hesitate to protect their assets. But wealthy women get the message loud and clear that they are lucky if any man will marry them because they are so intimidating—unless, of course, it's a man who *wants* their money. Remember that money equals power. And no man wants his ego trampled by a woman who has more money than he does. Is it any wonder that most women hesitate to rock the financial boat either before or during marriage?

All of this speaks to the whole issue of women and money and men. If a woman has more money, why shouldn't she protect it? But it's not a level playing field. Women compromise their own interests all the time. It goes back to the social conditioning of early childhood. No matter how successful women are or how much wealth they've accumulated, the message they've gotten over the years is to *keep the relationship at all costs.* Consequently women will figure out a way to make the shoes fit regardless of their discomfort.

If a woman who is financially set and is already familiar with the world of money has problems separating her money from her emotions, just think about the new investor who is taking charge of her finances for the first time.

If you are a new investor, you may feel intimidated and lack confidence because you just don't feel that you know enough. Consequently, when an investment doesn't work out, the old fear of "I can't 'do' money" rears its ugly head. It's as though a mysterious button has been pushed as you automatically lapse into your old way of thinking about money, the old litany of "I knew I couldn't do it. I shouldn't have even tried."

Many women discover that their investments become a reflection of their own self-worth. This shouldn't be. Men have known the truth for years:

Your money is a reflection of your net worth, not your self-worth.

This is why it's so much easier for men to cut their losses. They know that if the shoes don't fit, you don't shorten your feet—you just buy new shoes.

And the same holds true for investments. If you're losing money on an investment, don't *keep* losing money. Don't throw good money after bad. If an investment isn't working, let it go. Cut your emotional ties. Don't blame yourself. Investment mistakes are not life threatening, but they can be financially threatening if you don't know when to let go.

Again, I remind you that investing is not an exact science. Some investments that seemed perfectly sound in the beginning may not pan out for reasons beyond your control: war breaks out in the Persian Gulf, a crisis erupts in south-central Los Angeles, the economy goes into a deep recession and takes its time moving into a period of recovery—who knows?

My point is that anything can happen. Wall Street is littered with the bodies of so-called experts who "knew it all." Believe me, if it were possible to know it all, the experts would retire early and be sipping mai-tais in the South Pacific. To paraphrase an investment truism, the only sure thing about the market is that it fluctuates.

Investment failures are not a reflection of who you are as a person. They don't make you a failure. But if you choose to keep wearing them, they'll make you feel as uncomfortable as a pair of ill-fitting shoes!

Controlling Your Money Instead of Letting It Control You: Choosing Your Investment Strategy

One of the best ways to combat your fear of investment mistakes is to learn more about the world of finance. This includes deciding on the investment strategy or strategies that best suit you.

In the previous chapters you were introduced to the world of investments, and you understand that to create a portfolio, you don't have to shop 'til you drop. Now you need some basic background information on the mechanics of the financial markets.

TO MARKET, TO MARKET

How many of you know what they're talking about on the nightly news when they say, "The Dow is down"?

What I usually hear from new clients is, "What is the Dow? And if the Dow is down, why are my stocks up? I just don't get it!"

Let me explain. The Dow—that is, the Dow Jones Industrial Average (DJIA)—comprises the following thirty stocks:

GOODYEAR	AT&T	BOEING
MERCK	DU PONT	TEXACO
COCA-COLA	UNION CARBIDE	AMERICAN EXPRESS
ALLIED SIGNAL	EXXON	CHEVRON
PHILIP MORRIS	EASTMAN KODAK	BETHLEHEM STEEL
J. P. MORGAN	UNITED TECHNOLOGIES	CATERPILLAR
SEARS	DISNEY	WOOLWORTH
GENERAL ELECTRIC	ALCOA	GENERAL MOTORS
INTERNATIONAL PAPER	MINNESOTA MINING	IBM
MCDONALD'S	PROCTER & GAMBLE	WESTINGHOUSE

The Dow is simply a measure of how these thirty stocks have per-formed during that day—*always the same thirty*. If you don't own any of these stocks, when the Dow goes up, it doesn't mean your stock has gone up, too—although it might have.

Sometimes you'll hear "The Dow went up and the broader market went down." This means that only the average of the above thirty stocks was up, while most of the rest of the market was down. It's important to remember that the Dow is nothing more than the same thirty stocks reported on a daily basis. Sometimes they add or delete a stock to the Dow, but basically it's always the same group.

Unfortunately, not understanding what the Dow means can make you feel incompetent. A client will call in a state of frustration and say, "The market is up and my stock is down—why is that?!" She begins to doubt herself, feeling that if the market is up and her stock is down, she has obviously picked the wrong stock. She's having a knee-jerk reaction, and it doesn't serve her well. She might, out of panic, quickly sell her stock—only to have it go up several points two days later.

What good are the Dow and the other market averages? They are good overall market indicators—but not necessarily good represen-tations of your portfolio.

For example, the Dow is down thirty-nine points and you own stock XYZ. Although XYZ is not a part of the Dow, you could assume that your stock is down—but it isn't. In fact, that day XYZ is up one point.

Although the Dow Jones Industrial Average is the most commonly used benchmark in terms of evaluating how stocks did, remember that it isn't really an accurate representation. Besides the Dow Jones

Industrial Average, there is also the Dow Jones Transportation Average and the Dow Jones Utility Average. These two are nondiversified averages, focusing on specific industry groups.

One of the reasons investing seems like such an inexact science is that these types of benchmarks aren't necessarily accurate indicators, which adds to investment confusion. The market is a very big place and doesn't live or die by a group of thirty diversified stocks. Let's say that two stocks on the Dow, like Texaco and Chevron, have a really bad day. This can bring the average down. The Dow is a weighted average, and every stock on it does not have equal weight. One or two of these thirty, if heavily weighted, can greatly influence how the Dow is going to close for the day.

Standard and Poor's 500 (S&P 500). Like the Dow, the S&P 500 is another market average, not an actual place where securities are traded. It reports what five hundred selected stocks have done during the day. Most of these stocks are listed on the New York Stock Exchange.

Some of the stocks on the Dow are also on the S&P 500 and vice versa—they are not mutually exclusive. Clearly, the better indicator of how the broader market is doing is the S&P 500 rather than the Dow.

While the Dow and the S&P 500 are a "wrap-up" of how the market has performed, the actual stocks themselves are traded either on the floors of one of the exchanges or by telephone or computer.

New York Stock Exchange (NYSE). The largest securities exchange in the country, the NYSE is located on Wall Street in New York City. It's often referred to as the "Big Board," and there are specific requirements for a company to be listed on this exchange. The companies traded here are usually big ones with big market value. Many of them are household-name companies that we've all heard of, like Disney or PepsiCo.

American Stock Exchange (AMEX). This stock exchange is also located in New York City. It has fewer stocks listed than the NYSE and less stringent requirements for listing. Many oil stocks are listed on the AMEX.

Both the NYSE and AMEX are auction markets. This means that if there's a seller, there's a buyer on the other side of the trade. Often on the nightly news, as the newscaster reports on the market, you'll see people yelling at each other and waving their hands on the floor of the exchange. This is known as an "open outcry system," where buyers and sellers meet.

If you ask me to buy two thousand shares of AT&T for you, I will write a ticket and send it to the wire operator in my office, who will key it in to our trader on the floor of the exchange. This trader will then go to the AT&T post (literally a little post) on the floor of the exchange and will bid on two thousand shares of AT&T. It will be bought at the best offered market price unless the client has specified a limit price.

If it's a small enough order, typically one hundred shares or less, it goes through an automated system known as the "small order execution system" and is filled almost immediately.

Not every company can qualify to be listed on the NYSE or the AMEX. There are requirements, which include the earnings of the company, market capitalization, and the number of shareholders. A Big Board listing is considered prestigious but is certainly no guarantee of success.

Over-the-Counter Market (OTC) and National Association of Securities Dealers Automated Quotation System (NASDAQ). Smaller companies, particularly those just getting started, are not going to meet the listing requirements of the exchanges. Other companies prefer not to be exchange-listed. An alternative is for their stocks to be traded over the counter (OTC). OTC is a market for securities made up of dealers who may or may not be members of an exchange. OTC is not a place. It is mainly a market conducted over the telephone and is regulated by the National Association of Securities Dealers. NASDAQ is an automated information network that provides brokers and dealers with price quotations on OTC stocks.

With an OTC stock you have the potential for real growth if you pick the right stock. You probably won't receive dividends, however, because the company's earnings are typically reinvested in their business.

How can you tell if a stock is traded OTC? If the stock symbol is four letters or more, it's almost always an OTC stock. Fewer than four letters means that it's listed on one of the exchanges.

Liz Claiborne used to be an OTC stock with the symbol LIZC. The company is now listed on the NYSE and trades under the symbol LIZ.

Again, some companies choose to remain OTC although they may qualify for exchange listing. For example, Apple Computer started out as an OTC stock when it was a brand-new company and is still traded OTC. Apple may eventually apply for Big Board listing—or it may not.

MARKET ACTIVITY, CONDITIONS, AND PEOPLE

Some investment terms have become so much a part of our vocabulary that they're commonly used by investors and noninvestors alike. However, just because everyone uses them doesn't necessarily mean that everyone knows what they're talking about.

Bull and Bear Markets. "Bull" and "bear" are terms used to describe the direction of the markets as well as an investor's sentiment about the market. When you're bullish it means that you believe stock prices are headed up, so it's a good time to buy. A bull market is trending upward.

A bear is the opposite. When you're bearish it means that you believe stock prices are headed down, so it may be a good time to sell or to "sell short" (see "Long, Short, and Margin"). A bear market occurs when stocks are trending downward. Of course risk comes into play because there is no way to determine how high or how low the market is going to get and in which direction it's headed first.

Bulls and bears apply to the bond market, too. If you're bullish on bonds, you think interest rates are going down, so the price of bonds will go up. If you're bearish on bonds, you think interest rates are going up, so the price of bonds will go down.

Overbought and Oversold. When people think that stocks have gotten too expensive and are due for a downturn, they think the stock market is "overbought." People will start selling so they can lock in profits. "Oversold" is the opposite of overbought. When people think that the market is undervalued and is due for an upturn, they think it's oversold. People will start buying stocks.

Rally. In a rally the market is moving up in a very bullish way. The stock market and the bond market can both rally. There can be a rally just for a day or a sustained rally, which means the market is moving up over a period of days. Sometimes a rally occurs after the market has been fairly low or leveled out. Although a gain of three points doesn't make for a stock market rally, a gain of fifty points does.

Hot Tip. A hot tip is information that may influence you to buy or sell a stock. If you get a hot tip, make sure it's not material inside information unavailable to the public. If it is, acting on it could land you in deep legal trouble. If it isn't, consider carefully and remember how many hot tips turn into cold comfort.

Long, Short, and Margin. Being "long" means that you own something. If you are long one hundred shares of AT&T, it means you actually own the stock. When you are long a stock or bond, you want it to go up in price so you can make a profit.

"Selling short" is a little more complicated. When you short a stock it means that you're betting it will go down. You do this by borrowing stock that you don't own. The borrowing is done through a brokerage firm. Let's say at the time you borrow a stock it is $40 a share. Now it goes down to $30 a share. You go into the market and actually buy the stock for $30 to replace the stock you borrowed and sold when the stock was at $40. You've made a $10 profit on every share that you sold short. Your goal when you sell short is to replace what you borrowed at a cheaper price. Your profit is the difference between what you sold the stock for less what you paid to buy it back and replace the borrowed shares.

Short selling is aggressive and definitely risky. You have unlimited risk if the stock goes up instead of down since you have to make up the difference. If a $40 stock goes up to $50, you've lost $10 a share. You can hold on to your short position, hoping that the price will drop back down, but obviously your risk will keep increasing should the stock climb higher.

When you short a stock, you have to pledge collateral. This is called "buying on margin." If you're going to short $10,000 worth of stock, you have to come up with $5,000 in cash or $10,000 worth of securities. If your stock starts moving up instead of down, you'll have to meet a margin call—which means you'll be forced to pledge additional securities as collateral or come up with more money to maintain your short position.

If your stock continues to move in the wrong direction, and you can't put up any more money or securities as collateral, it will be bought back at the prevailing market price and you will have to cover the loss beginning with your initial collateral.

When you buy on margin, interest is charged by the brokerage firm at its margin loan rate, which can vary depending on the amount borrowed. Margin interest may be tax-deductible.

Risky Business

Short selling is *very* risky business—certainly not for the novice investor or the financially faint of heart. Likewise, these high-risk investments are better left to high rollers:

FUTURES AND COMMODITIES

Ironically, investing in commodities began with farmers trying to protect the future prices of their crops. Now it may well be the ultimate gambling investment. It's a bet on the future direction of a particular commodity or financial intrument. You can buy a futures contract on anything from gold to pork bellies, from U.S. government bonds to foreign currency. Futures are extremely risky, since you can lose even more than your initial investment because of margin calls—when you have to put up more money to maintain your position.

Personally, I've never traded commodities for myself or my clients, nor do I plan to. Although lots of stories are told about all the money that's made, the truth is that people consistently lose more than they make. Commodities and futures are for the very sophisticated trader with an extremely high-risk profile. (Notice I said trader, not investor.)

Huge amounts of money can be made and lost in a ten-minute time span.

This is definitely not the type of investment for any woman who is at once trying to deal with her fear of money and take charge of her financial life. If a woman asks me about commodities, I tell her about the risks involved and make it clear that this kind of trading is not what I consider investing—it's speculating.

Certain futures strategies can be profitable for sophisticated investors—especially for institutions like pension funds. You can buy futures on the S&P 500—which is a bet on the broader market's movement. This can be done to protect your portfolio and hedge your stock positions. It is all too involved for the beginning investor, however. For women who want a well-balanced growth and income portfolio, commodities aren't suitable.

PROGRAM TRADING

Since I brought up futures and commodities, I will mention program trading, which is a kind of adjunct to futures trading. It takes advantage of pricing discrepancies that occur between parallel markets. Program trading has nothing to do with fundamental stock investing and everything to do with technical short-term trading. It's typically used for very large portfolios like pension funds and other institutional investors.

Program trading works on the premise that sometimes it's cheaper to buy stock futures and sell a corresponding "basket" of stocks. This will drive stock prices downward. Conversely, when it's cheaper to buy stocks and sell the futures, program trading will impel stock prices upward. Program trading is done by computers that call out buy and sell signals either to buy the stock and sell the futures or sell the stock and buy the futures. You can see how program trading can account for a fair amount of volatility in the market.

Often when there are really wide price swings, it may not be started by program trading—but it certainly is exacerbated by program trading. Program trading can make an up day even better and a down day even worse. Institutional investors can benefit from program trading because it can protect large portfolios. But for the individual investor it's not quite so wonderful—it's easy to get caught in the fray.

PURCHASING OPTIONS, PUTS, CALLS, STRIKE PRICE, AND LEVERAGE

When you buy an "option," *you are buying the right* to buy or sell a specific stock at a specific price called the "strike price" for a limited, finite period of time. The strike price and expiration date of your option contract specify its particulars and affect its cost.

If you believe that ABC is going up, it's cheaper for you to buy an option on ABC than actually to buy the stock itself. To buy one hundred shares of ABC might cost you about $5,000—but to buy an option to control one hundred shares of ABC might only cost you $500 or less. Options provide a great deal of leverage because you can control a substantial amount of stock for a small amount of money.

If you buy a "call," you are bullish and believe a specific stock will go above a specific price within a specific period of time. When you buy a "put," you are bearish and believe that a specific stock will go below a specific price within a specific period of time.

An option is a vanishing or wasting asset because you own it only for a finite period of time. You have to sell or exercise your option on or before expiration. Once an option expires, it's worthless.

Most option buyers are prepared to lose their entire investment if they guess wrong. And if they're not, they should be.

VENTURE CAPITAL

Start-up businesses or businesses looking to expand typically require substantial infusions of cash, sometimes on an ongoing basis. Because banks and other conventional lenders often decline to make loans to such businesses (especially in recent years), they are forced to turn to investors for capital.

In return for providing venture capital, investors either receive profit participation, income in the form of interest payments, or both. Obviously, providing venture capital is very risky business. Depending on the success—or failure—of the particular company, you could end up backing the next superstar. Or the next superloser.

Market Strategies

There's more than one way to view the financial markets and several ways to approach investing. It's a matter of which one feels the most comfortable to you.

We've all heard about the financial whiz kids who profess to have the stock market all figured out. These experts and gurus tell the rest of us exactly what to do to make money. But does anyone *really* have it all figured out? I think not. Many of these market mavens have gone from hero to zero in less time than it takes to say "I told you so." Nevertheless, it's worth taking a look at their various market strategies if only to learn what *should* work but often doesn't.

GROWTH INVESTING

A growth investor, in terms of stock selection, looks for companies that are growing. Some companies report increasing earnings every year. These take the money that they would have paid out in dividends and put it back into developing the company. A growth investor's top priority is identifying companies that are in a strong growth mode.

VALUE INVESTING

A value investor looks at companies that are undervalued. These are companies that may have fallen out of favor. Their stock is cheap. Once the economy starts picking up, value investors may look at the companies that have been beaten up, whose stock prices are really low, and determine that they are undervalued. They start buying them while they are cheap on the premise that they'll appreciate rapidly as people get clued in to the fact that they represent value at a very low price.

INCOME INVESTING

If you're an income investor, you look at companies whose stocks pay high dividends. You are interested in stocks with higher than average income with lower than average price volatility.

CONTRARIAN INVESTING

If you are a contrarian investor, you are the ultimate value investor. You're looking at the stocks that have really sunk to the bottom of the barrel. Contrarians have the "straw hats in winter approach" to investing—they buy the stocks that everyone else hates. They take the value approach and stretch it as far as it will go. If you're a good contrarian, you have the ability to really sit with an investment. Having bought the great unloved, you're going to hold on until proven right.

SECTOR ROTATION

As a sector rotator, your emphasis is on pinpointing industries that will outperform the market as a whole. Let me explain: The market goes through rotations, meaning that at certain times certain types of stocks are in favor. Sometimes the health care stocks are in favor, and, as a sector, health care stocks do well.

If you are taking a sector rotation approach, you may buy last year's "dogs" on the premise that they'll be the leaders this year—because what goes around comes around . . . and goes back around. A good example: Biotech stocks were the stars in 1991. In early 1992 they were out of favor. Sector rotators would say: "Biotech has been leading in the past, so this sector is due to go out of favor. There will be a rotation out of biotech."

Sector rotators will then look for unloved sectors that they believe will come into favor. In many ways a sector rotator combines a value approach with a contrarian approach. You may rotate out of a "hot" sector into one that has underperformed.

MARKET TIMING AND MARKET TIMERS

Market timing is when you try to guess what the market is going to do next. Market timers are technicians who believe that they can anticipate what the market is going to do by observing the market itself, the direction of interest rates, and many other indicators. They actively trade their portfolios, buying when they think the market is due for an upturn and selling when they think the market is headed south.

ASSET ALLOCATION

Asset allocators use computer models and market timing. They use a number of different barometers to try to predict the relative value of stocks, bonds, and cash.

Asset allocators who were on the mark in 1987 rotated out of stocks before the October meltdown. They were able to do this because their asset allocation models called out an early warning signal, so they moved out of stocks and into cash.

The problem with asset allocation is that it often works better in theory than in practice. Not all asset allocators can translate what *should be* into what *is.*

BOTTOM-UP OR TOP-DOWN?

Within the general framework of any of these investment strategies, you can take a bottom-up approach or a top-down approach.

If you take a bottom-up approach, you are looking at individual companies. You evaluate Company XYZ based on the merits of Company XYZ. This is independent of what the overall economy is doing and independent of the broader market.

A top-down approach means that you begin by looking at the big picture, including the economic climate, market performance, and so forth. You then consider which companies will do well in this environment. If you take a top-down approach, you may invest in themes, like the aging of America. You will make your stock selections accordingly—in this case, perhaps choosing pharmaceutical companies that will benefit as the population ages and sales increase.

The logical application here in saying "If the shoes don't fit, don't shorten your feet" is that sometimes one of these approaches works, other times it doesn't. So rather than shorten your feet, hedge with more than one approach.

For example, my approach is a growth orientation. This is what I believe in. But since the shoes don't always fit, I hedge with value investments to balance out a portfolio. But I don't cut off my feet, which means that I still maintain a growth position.

If you use two different money managers, make sure they have different approaches. Invest some of your money with a growth manager and some with a value manager. This is a good use of diversification in your investment strategy. One manager should complement the other.

Let's assume that you are comfortable with a growth approach. In early 1992 this approach didn't work very well. But that didn't mean that you should bail out of all your growth stocks . . . and shorten your feet.

There are two alternatives. You could add value stocks to your portfolio to balance it out. Or, you could just hold on to your growth position because it's what you believe in for the long term.

FUNDAMENTAL ANALYSIS, TECHNICAL ANALYSIS, AND VALUE INVESTORS

There are two ways of evaluating a stock that you are considering buying. If you use fundamental analysis, you are studying the particulars of the company, including their product or service, their management, and their earnings. With technical analysis you look at the performance of the stock price over a period of time. Is the stock price trending up or is it trending down?

Technical analysts track the movement of stock prices on graphs, hoping to predict future stock prices. Pure technicians couldn't care less what the company does—whether it makes widgets or watches.

Fundamental analysts are less concerned with a stock's recent market activity than with the company's intrinsic value or worth. An undervalued company trading cheaply is a real "find." Their attitude is, "I don't care if no one's buying it, I'm pleased as punch that it's cheap because there's value here." They will be buyers because they are value investors.

Personally, I find both approaches profitable. I do a fundamental analysis first because if a company doesn't interest me, I'm not going to be a buyer. However, if I find a company that I really like, one that has a great product or service, has good earnings and good management, I will go ahead and do some technical analysis to see what the stock price has been historically and at what price it might make sense to buy.

What about Bonds?

Interest rate anticipation is used as an investment strategy for fixed-income investments like bonds. Managed bond portfolios are actively traded. Bonds are bought and sold and maturities are shortened or lengthened based on the direction of interest rates. When interest rates come down, bond prices go up. If interest rates do come down, you're going to have the biggest capital appreciation potential in long bonds.

So if you are bullish and believe that interest rates are going to come down, and you're very aggressive, you would buy thirty-year bonds. Conversely, if you expect interest rates to go up, you'll want to get out of the long side of the market and put your money in short-term financial instruments.

You can see how interest rate anticipation is used in bond or fixed income portfolios. Again, if you expect interest rates to go up, you want to be in short-term bonds. If you think interest rates are coming down, lock in long-term yields at today's higher interest rate for income and capital appreciation potential.

Two Investment Strategies That Always Work

You have just become acquainted with the various market strategies that could work, should work, and sometimes do work. Now let me introduce you to two investment strategies that *always* work.

DIVERSIFICATION, ASSET ALLOCATION, AND HEDGING

Diversification, also known as "asset allocation," basically means not to put all of your money in one investment (XYZ municipal bond) or one type of investment (*only* municipal bonds). Basically it means "Don't put all your eggs in one basket." Own a mix of stocks, bonds, money markets, and real estate, for example. The reason for this is that different types of investments do well in different economic environments. If you put every dollar in real estate, you could get killed financially in a recession. By not being diversified in your investments, you're taking the biggest risk of all because you have no "hedge"— nowhere to run, nowhere to hide. Hedging your risk means diversifying. It's like having something in your left hand in case what you have in your right hand doesn't work.

DOLLAR-COST AVERAGING

When you "dollar-cost average," instead of investing all of your money at one time, you invest an equal number of dollars at different times. Let's say that you want to invest $10,000 in McDonald's stock. You can invest $2,000 today, $2,000 next month, and so on. The price isn't going to be the same every time you buy it, so if the price goes down, you'll buy more shares; if the price goes up you'll buy fewer shares. In the end, your average cost may be less than it would have been if you'd invested all of your money at once. Buying securities this way means you don't have to be concerned about market timing.

In investment strategies when I say "If the shoes don't fit, don't shorten your feet," I'm talking about taking a position and holding it. Don't abandon what you believe in just because your approach isn't in vogue. Allow your comfort level to dovetail with your common sense—especially when it comes to investment strategies. You might be uncomfortable with your growth strategy because value investing is fashionable at the moment. But your common sense should remind you that what goes around comes around. So stay calm and stay tuned.

Be an Investor—Not a Trader

Again, we come back to the importance of keeping your emotions separate from your money. If your portfolio is down in the first quarter of the year, don't panic and allow your emotions to wipe out your investment strategy. Remember that when you're an investor, you're in for the long haul.

When a client starts to panic, I ask her: "Are your reasons for owning these investments still valid?" If she says yes, I tell her to sit tight. I ask if she's shifted her fundamental investment strategy, perhaps from a growth orientation to a value approach. If her answer is no, I advise her to leave well enough alone.

The best strategy of all, which takes us back to the discipline of the two Cs and two Ds, is sticking with your plan. Yes, you should revisit it at least quarterly and revisit it when you go through life changes. But let your common sense and comfort level work together here.

Market Timing versus Buy and Hold

"Buy and hold" is what we've just been talking about. Again, if you're a growth investor and your strategy didn't work too well during the first quarter of 1992, are you going to bail out of your growth stocks now? In my opinion, no. If you're a long-term investor and you still believe in your original strategy, if over the long term it has worked and you believe that ultimately it *will* work, I would not sell, I would hold. Buy it and leave it alone.

Most investors should allow themselves at least a two- to three-year time horizon for stock ownership.

If you're not a buy and hold investor, remember two things. First, in a nonretirement account, you're going to have tax ramifications every time you sell. You also may have a commission to pay every time you sell. A buy and hold strategy will cut down on commission costs as well as taxes.

Second, you will probably do a lot better in the long term with a buy and hold strategy.

A market timing strategy is a variation on a trading approach. Market timers are asset allocators. They're attempting to time the market and assess the relative value of each of the asset classes. They will move in and out of investments. I consider this trading, not investing. Is this a good idea? Yes, if you're right. If market timing got you out of stocks before the 1987 crash, then it was a good approach.

Unfortunately, most market timers are wrong more often than they're right. The real question is, who is really able to time the market? I have never been able to buy a stock at its low or sell a stock at its high—nor do I even try.

A client will ask me about a stock she likes that has really gotten beaten up. She wants to buy it, but first she asks me, "Do you think it will go lower?"

My answer is, "I don't know. What do you think?"

She wants a definitive yes or no, but I can't give her one. If this stock is $48 a share when she asks, I have no way of knowing if it will be down to $46 tomorrow or up to $50.

Truly, investing is a very humbling experience, because just when you think you have it all figured out, you find out you don't. And neither does anyone else. So I tend to be more of a buy and hold investor because I certainly don't claim to have market timing figured out.

Market timers assume that they can predict what the market will do next. If they buy something and then think it's going out of favor, they'll be out of it —they will shorten their feet.

Stop Loss

A "stop loss" order is a mechanism that is used to protect a profit or to minimize a loss. You buy stock ABC at $30 a share. It moves up to

$50 a share, which means you have a $20 per share profit to protect. Now let's assume you think ABC will go higher, but you don't want to jeopardize your profit—which could happen if the stock tumbles suddenly. What you can do is put a stop loss on your ABC stock and specify at what price you want to sell. A stop loss is always put in below the current market price. Since ABC is at $50, you could decide that you want to sell if ABC drops to $45 per share—or wherever your comfort level is.

There is no cost to enter a stop loss order unless your trade is executed. There are two important points, however: When you specify a stop loss price, it is not necessarily the price that you'll sell at. If you say you want to be stopped out of ABC at $45, when ABC trades at $45 you are entitled to the next trade. Let's assume that the next trade on ABC is $44⅞—that's the price you'll get stopped out on. Or, if you get lucky, the next trade could be higher. So it's not the price you specify, but the next trade after that.

It's also important to know that although a stop loss protects your profit and curtails a loss, there is always the chance that you'll get stopped out and the stock will go right back up that same day. For instance, stock ABC hits your stop at $45, so you get stopped out. But before the end of the day ABC rebounds to $48. This means you've gotten out with some profit but may wish that you were still in.

So think before entering a stop loss. You may want to use it with higher-risk stocks, where there's a lot of volatility. Remember, though, that a stock may have a bad run for a few days and then move right back up. You'll want to set a stop loss not less than 10 percent below the current market price—in fact, 15 percent is probably more reasonable.

Allow your stock some breathing room. If you set the stop price too close to the market price, your chances of getting stopped out quickly are much greater.

You can also use a "trailing stop." As the stock moves higher, you can reset your stop loss price as well. This way you're following the stock price up. You cancel the previous stop loss and reenter a new, higher stop loss price. This is a good way to "readjust" your investment—a very good way to keep the same shoes without shortening your feet.

When the Shoes No Longer Fit

Let's say you have a balanced growth and income portfolio. But because you're older you need more income than growth. Your shoes don't fit anymore—but that doesn't mean you have to cut off your feet. All you have to do is shift some of your growth investments to income investments to compensate because your feet may have gotten a bit wider as you've gotten a bit older.

The opposite is true if you're still having babies. If you have mostly income-oriented investments in your portfolio and decide to become pregnant, shift some of that income to growth for inflation protection. With pregnancy, you may find high heels less comfortable, so try wearing lower heels sometimes. Think about the growth that stocks will provide by the time your baby is ready for college.

The Esther Berger
Tried-and-True Chicken Approach to Investing

What if you can't decide if you're bullish or bearish? How about being chickenish? Let's assume that LMN has gone way up and I have a nice profit to protect. I may sell half my shares and hold the other half. If the stock price falls, that's okay because I've taken a nice profit on half my investment. If it goes up, I'm not going to get upset because I still own it and I'm making more profit.

This is similar to dollar-cost averaging on the sell side. Instead of investing at regular intervals, you're selling to take a profit.

Tax Losses, Mutual Fund Switches, and the Wash Sale Rule

A wash sale is a provision in the tax code that extends a tax benefit to an investor who sells an investment at a loss. However, if the investor buys back the same investment, or a substantially similar investment, within thirty days, the IRS deems the original sale a "wash sale" and the tax loss is negated.

Let's assume that you sell QRS at a loss. If it's not in a retirement plan, you can take a tax loss. Fifteen days go by. QRS goes up, you decide that you should never have sold it, and you buy back QRS. Your loss won't count for tax purposes because you bought it back before thirty days had elapsed. It's as if you never sold it, and you won't get to take the loss. Only on day thirty-one can you buy it back and take the loss.

This applies to mutual fund switches as well. When investors switch from one mutual fund to another, *even within the same fund family,* it's a taxable event (if it's not in a retirement plan). If they switch back into the same fund before thirty days have elapsed, they can't take the tax loss, if there is one. This was a tragedy for many investors in October 1987, when the one silver lining might have been a tax loss. One of my husband's clients switched from a stock fund into a money market fund on the day of the crash. Two days later she felt that stocks would rebound and went right back into the original stock fund. She wiped out her tax loss. She was heartbroken when my CPA husband had to be the bearer of bad tidings.

When should you consider selling or switching to another fund? When something material changes in your reason for owning it. Maybe the fund manager has left and the new manager is an unknown. Do you want to give the new manager a chance or get out altogether? It's a judgment call at best.

Or let's assume you own a gold mutual fund but suddenly stop believing in gold as a good inflation hedge. Or perhaps you discover something that you didn't know about your mutual fund. Maybe you own a bond fund and then find out the manager is writing options against the portfolio. You thought you were in a plain vanilla government fund, only to learn that it was much more complicated. It's not what you thought it was—it's potentially riskier. As with other investments, it never hurts to revisit your mutual fund and confirm that your reasons for owning it are still valid and that it is still compatible with your financial objectives and risk tolerance.

Maybe you are in a stock mutual fund, are about to retire, and will need more income. You'll want to consider switching to an income-oriented fund.

Mutual funds, by definition, are longer-term investments. You don't want to trade mutual funds aggressively, and you don't want to use market timing with mutual funds.

Knowing How to Take a Tax Loss

Let's assume that you've made some big profits during the year. What you may want to do is sell some of the "losers" in your portfolio so you can offset the gains with the losses. Talk to your CPA or tax attorney before making any decisions. The way the tax law works *currently* is that you can use capital losses against capital gains dollar for dollar. This means if you have $5,000 in gains, you can offset them with $5,000 in losses. If you've got more losses than gains, you can use $3,000 of tax losses against ordinary income in any one tax year and carry the loss forward year to year until it is used up. You can use the loss indefinitely.

Let's assume you have $5,000 worth of gains and $10,000 worth of losses in 1992. The first $5,000 of losses is used dollar for dollar against your gains. You can use an additional $3,000 against ordinary income for 1992. The following year, 1993, you can use the remaining $2,000 against ordinary income, although before you use it against income you'll use it against any capital gains for that year.

When you sell for tax purposes, you don't have to limit yourself to selling stocks. You might also consider a bond swap. As with any investment, when you're taking a loss for tax purposes, don't buy back the same bond within thirty days. But you can buy a similar bond, perhaps one with a different issuer or with a slightly different maturity or coupon rate. It must be different enough so you can take the tax loss.

When selling for tax purposes, always sell the weakest links in your portfolio—the investments that deserve to be sold based on their merits (or lack thereof). Sell those investments that never should have been bought in the first place, either because they didn't make sense or because you weren't comfortable with them from the get-go.

But don't sell the investments that still work. Why shorten your feet if the shoes fit just fine?

I HAVE ALL MY MONEY IN MUTUAL FUNDS. IS THAT A GOOD IDEA?

Maybe. That depends on what kind of mutual funds you own. Like stocks and bonds, mutual funds come in all shapes and sizes, ranging from money markets to global bond funds. A mutual fund is a professionally managed portfolio where many investors' dollars are pooled together. The fund manager does all the buying and selling and is the hands-on decision maker. It may be a good idea to have all your money in mutual funds. An even better idea is to make sure you've thoroughly investigated the funds and the fund managers before you invest.

Secret #9 . . .

Never Marry an Investment:
Knowing When to Buy and Sell

Janet, twenty-six, came to me for investment advice after inheriting an extensive investment portfolio from her eighty-year-old grandfather. As I reviewed her new holdings, I pointed out that many of the investments weren't appropriate for her. They just didn't fit with her twenty-six-year-old life-style.

At first she wouldn't listen to me; she kept repeating, "But my grandfather left them to me. He worked very hard for sixty years. I'll never sell his stocks—I mean, how can I?"

She was glaring at me across my desk as though I were suggesting that we dig up his body and take out his teeth for the gold! I know this sounds funny—but that's how attached some women get to their investments.

Then there's Linda, whose husband, Stephen, divorced her three days before her forty-second birthday. The portfolio she received in the divorce settlement was not suitable for her needs. Stephen had been an aggressive investor—far more aggressive than Linda was prepared for. Most of the holdings were penny stocks and junk bonds of dubious value.

As I pointed this out to her and suggested changes that needed to be made immediately, her response was, "Stephen always handled our finances and planned everything so that the kids and I would always be taken care of. How could he have done this?"

Luckily for Linda, Janet, and all of us, financial decisions are not "till death do us part." The old saying "If it ain't broke, don't fix it" in the investment world is "If it's broke, fix it fast!"

You were married to your husband. And in a sense, as a daughter you were married to your father. *But you're not married to your investments.*

Before You Sell, Understand What You Own and Why

Every time you make an investment, including money markets, CDs, and even just plain savings accounts, you should have a reason. Let's assume you have your money in a money market or in a bank account. Your reasons could be:

- You don't know what else to do with it, and it feels safe and familiar there.

- You're going to need to touch that money soon . . . so you need to keep it liquid.

- You have no risk tolerance whatsoever, so you need to keep it completely safe.

- You think that interest rates are going up and you want to keep your money in cash so that if you're correct, you can lock in higher yields.

Revisiting every investment in your portfolio and making sure that your reasons for buying each investment are still intact is a good starting point for portfolio updating. When your reasons for owning a particular investment no longer hold true, it's time for you to make a change.

Let's assume that you have a well-diversified portfolio. You've got some cash, some stocks, and some bonds. But before you talk about how to move out of any investment, you should understand why you got in. This means applying the commonsense part of the two Cs and two Ds.

Everything in your portfolio needs to have a reason. Most people go wrong in investing because they don't have a well-defined reason for investing in something. I often hear the same reasons for this: "It just seemed like a good thing to do." "Someone suggested that I do it." "I read about it somewhere." But the key to good financial planning is understanding why you own every investment in your portfolio.

Now we just discussed different reasons for having your money in cash. What about stocks? Any of the following reasons are valid for owning stocks:

- Growth . . . you're reaching for higher returns.

- You have some tolerance for risk and you have an appetite for something other than money markets offering complete safety.

- You want to keep pace with inflation, and you understand that over time inflation will erode the purchasing power of your portfolio.

- Someone gave you a stock tip, and *after careful research,* you really believe that it will pan out.

And for bonds:

- You need the interest income from the bonds to supplement your income.

- Your portfolio is heavily weighted with common stocks, so you need bonds to help you strike a balance.

- You're buying long-term bonds that will mature when you retire.

- Bonds make you feel safe and let you sleep better at night.

Understanding why you own any investment is ultimately going to be your tickler in terms of when you need to sell.

Some Valid Selling Points

Let's assume you bought a stock for growth and it has grown and is doing nicely. But now you're near retirement age and you need less growth and more income in your portfolio. It makes sense to sell some of your growth stocks and buy bonds for the income they will provide.

Or you may decide to sell certain investments because there has been a fundamental change in the economic environment. What made sense in the go-go 1980s may not make sense in the slow-grow 1990s.

Or you may need to sell because of life changes you're going through. There may have been a family crisis, so you can no longer afford to take as much risk with your capital because you need safety. You may have to liquidate a stock because you're faced with a financial emergency and you need the money now. You may move out of stocks because you've lost your job, which means you can't afford to take any risk; you need more security.

Then there's the good news: you've just received an inheritance. Up until now most of your money has been in bonds because you needed safety and income. Although you may decide not to sell any of your bonds because you bought them when interest rates were high, you can certainly use your newfound wealth to add stocks to your portfolio for growth.

Let's say that the stock market is very cheap and you perceive value in it. You may want to sell some of your bonds and shift into stocks. The flip side could be that you perceive the stock market as very risky because it's run up quite a bit. You may want to move out of stocks. If you're not sure how you want to invest, you may want to place your investment dollars temporarily in a money market or in a short-term CD until you decide what to do.

In each of these scenarios, the economy, the financial market, or a life change dictates that you consider selling certain investments and replacing them with others that are more appropriate.

But what about when an investment itself changes?

You may have invested in a particular stock because you believed in the chief executive officer of the company. Under his tutelage, the company grew in leaps and bounds and the stock went up, up, up!

Suddenly the CEO, who you believe is responsible for the company's growth, is leaving the company. Your reason for owning that stock no longer holds true because you bought it for the specific reason that you believe this CEO is a dynamo. You're going to sell while you can still take a nice profit because you have no idea what will happen to the company when the new CEO takes over.

Your decision to sell is not a function of the economy, the financial market, or a change in your life-style. You're selling because your specific reason for owning this specific investment is no longer intact.

You may choose to sell because you object to something a company is doing. This is often the case if you're a socially responsible investor.

Jeanine owned the stock of a well-known company that manufactures personal care products. But when she read in a business magazine that the company tests its products on laboratory animals, she was furious.

She called and told me to sell the stock immediately. It didn't matter that it was down two points since she'd bought it—she wanted out no matter what. Jeanine told me, "Esther, I'm in the market to make money, but not at the cost of what I believe in. Let's find another investment that I can live with, because this one doesn't work for me."

Selling to Take a Quick Profit

A very disciplined investor is looking for a specific rate of return. Again, let's go back to using Treasuries as a benchmark. If Treasuries are yielding 4 percent, and you're getting a 12 percent return on a stock investment, you should be pleased as punch because you're getting three times the return on Treasuries.

If you buy a stock that's very aggressive—in the top tier of the money triangle—you're looking for maximum capital appreciation. You may get lucky and have a 20 percent gain in two months and believe that there's potential for even more. Personally, I'd take the 20 percent and run. I'm not going to be a pig! Remember that with stocks, what goes up comes down. So if you've got a quick profit, take it.

Understand that you're never going to call a market top or a market bottom. That's why the saying on Wall Street is: "Bulls and bears make money. Pigs get slaughtered!"

Annualizing your return can help you decide if it's time to take a profit. For example, if you have a 20 percent return in a two-month period of time, annualize it by multiplying by six (2 months x 6 = 12 months). This gives you a 120 percent annualized return. Hard to argue with taking a profit here!

Although my approach to investing is buy and hold, I will never disagree with a client who wants to take a substantial profit after a very short period of time. If there's a big run-up in the bond market because of declining interest rates, I can't argue if someone calls up and says, "You know, I've got a nice profit here—I don't want to be a pig. I'm going to sell."

You'll hear on the nightly news, "Stocks were down today in a round of profit taking. . . ." This means people have made money and aren't going to stick around and be pigs. They're going to take their money off the table. This is not a bad thing to do.

There is another adage on Wall Street: "Buy the rumor, sell the news." For instance, when there is a pharmaceutical company applying for FDA approval on a new drug, the stock may run up in anticipation of FDA approval. Then, when the approval is announced, and it's good news, frequently the stock will drop from profit taking. People bought it, it went up, and now they're taking profits.

When to Hold and When to Fold

Psychology and momentum affect much of the buying and selling in the financial markets. What other people are doing influences many investors. A little bit of panic can create a lot of chaos and make people start selling when they shouldn't be.

Always resist the temptation to follow the crowd. It's a good idea to understand the ins and outs of every investment that you own and remember why you bought it in the first place. If one of your favorite stocks suddenly heads south, it could be for any number of reasons:

- It could be an economically sensitive stock, and bad news about the economy came out that will affect the company negatively.

- There may be something wrong with the company itself—they reported earnings that were much worse than expected.

- It could be that investors are just taking profits.

When should you consider selling? If there's bad news about the company or if the economy is going to affect your company negatively, meaning the stock may be down in the basement for a while. But if it's just a round of profit taking, you have a choice to make. You can take your profits along with everybody else, or you can stick around and possibly buy more if the stock moves down farther. Also, if the profit taking has already happened and the price is already down, you don't really want to sell because you probably missed the move. Don't sell just when the stock may be due for a rebound.

When it comes to taking a profit, don't make the mistake of letting the tail wag the dog. This means you should not refuse to take a profit because you are going to have to pay tax on it. That's a less than valid reason for holding on to an investment.

Yes, taxes are very important. *However,* your decision has to be based on investment merit first, not tax considerations. To pay a capital gains tax means you had to have made money. And what's wrong with that?

Some people have the attitude of "No, I'm not going to sell because by the time I pay taxes . . ." Well, that's not valid. There *is* a silver lining to paying taxes. Again, it means that you made money. It's as simple as this: Don't be afraid to sell and take a profit because you don't want to pay taxes. At the risk of sounding Pollyannaish, paying taxes means you're successful. That's something to be proud of.

By not selling and taking a profit, you could eventually end up losing more than you would have paid in taxes if your stock should suddenly drop. Once again, this is about not being a pig!

If the entire stock market is down, as in October 1987, or if the entire bond market is down because interest rates have gone way up, you have a decision to make. There is something out there that's affecting every investment in a particular asset class. Do you want to be out of bonds altogether because your reason for buying them is no longer valid? Perhaps you bought bonds in anticipation of lower interest rates—now rates are going higher, so you want to move out of bonds.

There may also be a particular problem with your stock or bond. For example, if you've got a substantial loss in XYZ stock when most stocks are performing very well, that may be a good reason to consider selling. But if everybody is in the same boat and your stock is doing about as well (or as poorly) as most others, this wouldn't necessarily impel you to sell unless you think that stocks are just not the place you should be right now.

In 1987 the whole stock market went down. Some people sold because they thought stocks would go even lower and they just wanted to be out of stocks altogether. It's not that their stocks were doing worse than any others.

But in a good market when stocks are going up, if yours are consistently going down—you'd better be asking why. Find out if there is something fundamentally wrong with the company. If so, you may want to take your loss and get out. But if everything is going down, and your stocks are going down about as much as the market—or at least not too much worse—you may want to hold on for the long term. Stocks tend to run up and then go back down again. They generally don't go up in a straight line but "consolidate" before they move higher. So if a stock runs up, it will typically come down a bit, consolidate, and form a "base." This means it levels off a bit before it starts its next climb.

If you do decide to sell, the important point is to take a loss while it's still reasonable. Remember when I talked about a stock going from $10 to $5 and then having to double to get back up to $10 again? What you have to do, depending on how disciplined you are, is define your risk tolerance.

If your stomach can take no more than a 20 percent loss and your stock is down 20 percent, then you've got a decision to make. If the whole market is down 20 percent, you may decide to swallow hard and stick around. But if the market is up and your stock is down 20 percent, you've reached what I consider to be your pain threshold.

You may very well want to be out and take the loss. You want to stay close to your comfort level and your discipline at this point.

Again, the two Cs and two Ds come back into play. You don't want your loss steamrolling to 30 percent, 40 percent . . . to the point when all you've got left is a tax loss. So you must be disciplined about protecting your down side. Personally, the big question mark for me is, if everything in the same asset class is down, am I willing to stick around or do I want to get out? This is where risk tolerance comes into play.

In 1987, when everything was down, most people had reached their 20 percent tolerance for pain. I told most of my clients, "This is how you can decide whether to sell or to hold. Your stock has dropped about as much as the market. Now you've got a decision to make. If you can hold on for the long term, I think you'll make your money back and be in a profit position by next year, or certainly two years out. If your stomach can't handle it, and if you can't deal with stocks possibly going lower before they go higher, then you need to be out." This was a critical decision for many investors at a time when they had to confront their common sense, comfort level, and discipline head on.

When stocks are down, the questions to ask yourself are "Can I tolerate more loss?" and "What's my maximum pain threshold?" For some people it's 10 percent, for some it's 20 percent. There is no right answer. The right answer is whatever is right for you.

Stock Psychology: Oversold or Overbought?

It's a good thing a stock isn't human. Over the course of its "lifetime," it puts up with a lot of abuse.

Sometimes a stock is sold to the point where it's oversold. When this happens, selling has depressed the stock price to a point where it is almost too low and there is actually more value in the company than its share price reflects.

Every company has an intrinsic worth, or "book value." This is the real worth of the company. Sometimes, however, stocks get so beaten up that they're selling too cheaply. If enough people dump a stock, they're going to drive the share price down so low that it becomes undervalued. If you can identify a stock when it's oversold, this can be a very good time to buy.

The flip side is when a stock gets overbought. Sometimes people will start bidding up the price of a stock and it goes up so high that its shares are selling for much more than the company is worth. Stocks trading too richly are poised for a fall. Sooner or later people are going to wake up and realize that they are paying a ridiculous price for a company that is not worth it. If you're holding a stock that is overbought, hope that you wake up before everyone else does so that you can take your profit while it's still there for the taking.

Time Is Money

Let's not forget about the "time value" of your money. In simple English: During the time that you're investing your money in a particular investment, could it be doing better elsewhere?

Let's assume you own ABC stock, which has underperformed while the rest of the market has been doing well. There are some specific problems with the company, but the situation is improving. Will ABC turn around? Possibly. But, again, consider the time value of your investment. Where else could your money be invested, and what could it be earning in the time it takes for ABC to turn around?

In a virtually no-risk money market, it will earn about 3 percent in the next year. If it stays in ABC, it may or may not make 3 percent. Are you willing to take that risk? Obviously, when interest rates are higher, investors are less inclined to take the risk of staying with an underperforming stock. If you can earn 7 to 8 percent in a money market (as you could several years ago), you may want to sell your stock and take your loss. But if the alternative is a 3 percent money market, you may want to sit tight if you still believe in the validity of your stock investment.

Every asset class has an average rate of return. This is not my opinion—it's based on historical fact. Stocks average about a 10 to 12 percent annual return; bonds about 5 to 6 percent. Remember, this is an average. Some years these returns are quite a bit higher, some years they are in minus territory. But they are good guidelines for assessing the time value of alternative investments.

In the early 1990s CD investors went into "sticker shock" when one-year CD rates came down below 4 percent. Many people moved out of CDs, saying, "I'm not going to sit around in CDs for the next year at under 4 percent when I could conceivably be making 10 to 12 percent in stocks." This is a valid argument as long as these investors remember that CDs and stocks are not apples and apples; they are apples and oranges—and sometimes lemons! If you're prepared to take more risk, fine. If not, stick to CDs.

Again, when you shift from investment A to investment B, part of what you need to think about is the time value of your money. *What could it be earning elsewhere in the same period of time?*

If you think it's going to take a particular stock a year to start moving up, would you rather have your money in something else that could be doing better during the next twelve months? Bear in mind, too, that dividends are not etched in stone. If a company is really in trouble, it may cut its dividend or stop paying dividends altogether.

There is also an overlap you should be aware of: time value blended with risk tolerance blended with taking a loss. A good example: A couple of years ago many investors bought mutual funds that invested primarily in Europe. Because of all the excitement about German reunification and the potential for the European Economic Community, the prognosis for European investments seemed excellent. But perception hasn't equaled reality, at least not yet.

Many investors have elected to get out of European investments because of the time value concept. They are taking losses and moving on, hoping to do better elsewhere rather than wait for their investment to turn around. Are they right or wrong? Will the European market turn around this year? Next year? In five years?

This is precisely the time value concept blended with risk tolerance blended with taking a loss. It also overlaps with common sense—the reason for buying the investment in the first place: you were bullish on Europe. Well, now you're not so bullish, you've got a 20 percent loss, and the time value of your money dictates that it could be better invested elsewhere. These are all valid reasons for taking a loss and making a change.

Putting It All Together

It's important to understand how all these things work together. There are many variables when you decide whether to sell an investment. A number of elements come into play, including time value, common sense, comfort level, and discipline.

To backtrack and make it simple:

- Look at the overall economy. How will it affect your investment?

- Look at the specific investment. Is there a problem you should know about?

- Revisit your reasons for owning the investment in the first place. Are they still valid?

- How comfortable are you holding on to this investment?

- Consider the time value of your investment. Where else could it be invested, and what could it be earning?

Also, always remember that there is never a right time to sell. Nobody calls market tops and nobody calls market bottoms—at least not correctly! Your guess is as good as anyone else's. And to some extent, that's just what it is—a guess.

My Chicken Approach Revisited

Again, let's look at the Esther Berger chicken approach to investing: I have a client, Sarah, with a very large portfolio, including $200,000 in long bonds—thirty-year Treasuries. She bought them for a specific reason: she believed that interest rates were going to come down, and long bonds do the best when rates come down (the longer the maturity, the more potential for appreciation). Sarah has a large profit in these bonds, annualized at about 30 percent. She's owned the investment for only three months. Sarah asked me if interest rates would go lower. Good question. Obviously no one knows for sure. Not me. Not Sarah. Not even the most respected market maven on Wall Street.

I suggested that she sell half her bonds and take profits and hold on to the other half so if rates do go lower, she could realize even more profit. If they don't go lower, Sarah has already taken some nice profits and she still owns some top-quality bonds that are paying very good interest.

Again, it's never going to be a clear-cut decision, and there are no guarantees—but especially if you're holding a large position, consider selling half. This way you'll be at least half-right and at most half-wrong. That's a pretty good way to hedge. Let's apply this to taking a loss: Maybe ABC stock *will* rebound this year. If you'd like to believe that it will but aren't thoroughly convinced, consider selling half your position and holding on to the rest on the chance that it will rebound.

Some people hesitate to sell because of transaction costs. Like taxes, brokerage commissions are relevant, and they do factor into your profit. But, just like taxes, brokerage commissions shouldn't be the tail wagging the dog. If selling an investment makes sense, don't make a decision *not* to sell just to avoid transaction charges. If you don't sell because you don't want to be paying a brokerage commission, your investment could go down far more than the cost of the commission itself.

Again, transaction charges are relevant and they are important. But again, they shouldn't be the tail wagging the dog.

Same Question, Different Answer

Different investors may own the same investment for very different reasons. And because their investment objectives are different, the same question—"I have a profit: should I sell?"—can have two very different answers.

For example, when clients invest for retirement, we often use zero-coupon Treasuries as a starting point. These are Treasuries that come in various maturities, and you can buy them to come due when you retire. They don't pay current interest. You buy them at a discount and you get back par value ($1,000 per bond) at maturity. If a client says,

"I need $200,000 in the year 2003," we can buy zeros today to get her that amount at retirement.

Now let's assume that interest rates come down considerably and my client, Naomi, has a huge profit on her zeros. Zeros are extremely sensitive to interest rate changes and typically appreciate more than coupon bonds when interest rates come down.

Naomi is excited about the profit on her zeros. But I have to remind her that she didn't buy them to make a profit. She bought them to have retirement money available in the year 2003, and she needs to have the security of having that money in 2003. So although she has a substantial profit, she should hold on to her zeros because her reason for buying them is still intact.

Now let's take a look at another investor, Teri, who bought the same bonds strictly for capital appreciation because she believed interest rates were going way down and the price of her zeros would go way up. If her reason for investing was to make a profit when rates come down, it's entirely valid for her to sell when she achieves her objective. She has good reason for selling and taking her profit. Unlike Naomi, Teri's objective was not to have the money come due in 2003: it was to make money now. Same investment, different objective.

Again, go back to your original reason for investing. The more well defined your reason for buying, the easier it will be to make a decision about selling. This is where discipline comes in. If you need that money in 2003, you don't want to sell to take a profit today even though it may be very tempting to do so.

Would You Buy It Today?

When you think about selling an investment, another good question to ask yourself is, "Would I buy it today at today's price?"

Let's say you bought XYZ stock at $30 a share, you still own it, and now it is trading at $50 a share. Would you buy it today at $50? If your answer is no, then it's a good indication that you think the stock is pricey and overbought. It may be time for you to sell. But if you think it still looks cheap at $50, why sell? Why not buy more?

Now let's assume that you also own ABC and it's really gotten beaten up, but you don't want to sell because you don't want to take a loss. Ask yourself, "Would I buy ABC right now? Is it a good investment?" If your answer is no, then why are you keeping a stock that you wouldn't want to buy? And if it's not worth buying today, why not sell it? If you don't think ABC is going to do well, remember the concept of time value and use your common sense. Why hold on to it? Don't be worried about taking a loss here.

It's never a mistake to clean up your portfolio—to weed out anything that's too aggressive, doesn't make sense, or never belonged there in the first place. It's fine to hold on to good-quality investments even when they're down, but don't hold on to your true losers until you've lost everything.

Now It's Mine, What Do I Do with It?

When you "inherit" a portfolio either through divorce or through an actual inheritance, don't assume you have to sell everything—or anything. First you have to evaluate every investment individually and ask yourself, "Does this work for me?" Take into consideration your age, your life-style, your financial goals, and your risk tolerance. It's no longer someone else's portfolio—now it's yours.

In most cases some changes will need to be made to make the portfolio fit who you are. You are not your ex-husband, your father, your grandfather, your mother, or your aunt Blanche. You are you. Your portfolio should be a statement of who you are financially. The investments in it should reflect *your* investment objectives.

If you're a single, twentysomething woman, chances are you're going to have a much different life-style from your eightysomething grandfather. If you inherit his portfolio, doesn't it make sense that you may need to make some changes?

Your emotional attachment to the person who originally owned your portfolio doesn't justify your owning something that really doesn't suit you. The pivotal question here is, "Is this something I would invest in today?" If your answer is, "No way!" then why should it stay in your portfolio? Sentiment? Emotional attachment? Wrong reason. Because it works for you and is a good investment is the only right reason.

To be a successful investor, your money has to steer clear of your emotions. Make financial decisions with your head, not your heart. The goal is to meet your investment objectives. Anything that doesn't do that isn't right for you.

Don't Divorce a Good Thing

We've talked a lot about never marrying an investment. But it's equally important never to divorce a good thing. If your ex-husband, Phil, managed the family investments wisely, and you've received a top-quality, well-diversified portfolio as part of your divorce settlement, don't get rid of the investments just because you can't stand Phil. I don't care how much you dislike your ex-husband. Don't dump investments that work just because the marriage didn't.

If you have an emotional response to any investment, recognize it for what it is. If you live in California and just can't bear to part with the Ohio municipal bond that your grandmother left you; if you hate top-performing XYZ stock just because your ex loved it—understand that you're not being logical. It's okay to feel the way that you do; it's just not the best way to go about investing. If you need to let your emotions dictate your investment decisions, that's your choice. After all, it's your money.

But if your objective is to *make* money, try hard to filter out the emotion. Every investment should make sense financially. It should not be distorted by sentiment. If you do have an emotional response to a particular investment, recognize what it is. Be honest about it.

Of course the best of both worlds is when an investment is emotionally gratifying *and* is also good, commonsense investing.

That's the ultimate twofer.

PART FOUR

Your Retirement Years: The Best Is Yet to Be

HOW CAN I GET INCOME FROM MY INVESTMENTS?

$ To structure a well-diversified income portfolio properly, consider using a mix of high-quality bonds, preferred stocks, utility stocks, and high-yield common stocks (not to be confused with high-yield junk bonds). For inflation protection—to hedge against the erosion of your purchasing power—you will need to include some growth stocks as well.

Secret #10 . . .
Growing Poor Safely Can Be Hazardous to Your Wealth: Investing in Yourself

I have a sixty-one-year-old client named Margaret who has all of her pension money invested in CDs. This includes every single penny of $533,000!

The first time I asked her why, she told me, "Because that's what I've always done. I don't want to make any changes. I've always done well with CDs." To every suggestion I made about diversifying and inflation-proofing her portfolio, Margaret just shook her head. She is adamant about keeping her money entirely in CDs, much to her financial detriment.

Margaret believes that she is handling her money wisely. There are no investments to understand, no commissions to pay. Basically, she doesn't have to do anything. So every night Margaret goes to bed feeling safe and secure, because her future is tucked away in CDs.

What Margaret doesn't realize is that CDs are extremely sensitive to interest rates. And in 1992 interest rates reached their lowest point in sixteen years. Margaret's retirement portfolio, which started out years ago in 10 percent CDs, is now rolling over at yields lower than 4 percent.

Although it's possible to lock in a high yield initially when interest rates are high, when a CD matures it can roll over at a much lower interest rate. And these days it certainly does. Indeed, in 1992, as billions of dollars' worth of CDs matured, investors experienced the financial world's equivalent of sticker shock—low, low, low interest rates.

There are lots of investors like Margaret, who have always invested "safely" in CDs—many of them because they have no idea where else to invest their money. Bonds are too confusing, and stocks seem much too risky. So they just let those CDs roll over and over at lower and lower interest rates.

What does this mean in real dollar terms?

With inflation currently running about 4 percent, it means that your money is worth 4 percent less this year than it was last year. And it will be worth even less next year. Unless Margaret changes her investment strategy, or interest rates suddenly move up (which usually means an even higher rate of inflation), by the time Margaret is in her midseventies she'll have a nice dollar amount with lots of zeros. But how much is it actually going to be worth? How much will it really buy? Will she be able to take her Caribbean cruise every year, maintain her second home in Florida, and enjoy all the other luxuries to which she's become accustomed?

Even at sixty-one, the financial realities of retirement haven't set in for Margaret. She still earns a hefty paycheck as president of a consulting firm and feels secure in knowing that over $500,000 is already in the bank. But it is a false sense of security.

Margaret hasn't stopped to think about the taxes she'll be paying when she withdraws her money from her pension plan. And once she factors in inflation, her "safe" investment will dwindle to much less than she imagined having during her retirement years as she slowly loses purchasing power.

Loss of purchasing power can be devastating because it happens gradually over a long period of time and may go unnoticed from year to year. The only thing you become aware of is that things seem to get a little bit tighter each year. But you still try to squeeze by. By the time you realize that you need to make major financial adjustments, it's almost too late.

Playing it safe doesn't always equal playing it smart. Keeping all your money in CDs (like Margaret), Treasuries, and money markets is a great way to *grow poor safely*.

Unfortunately, many sixtysomething women are drawn to these types of investments because they are accessible, familiar, and easy to understand. Although they may help you feel confident about your investment ability, they don't make good sense 100 percent of the time for 100 percent of your dollars. As I've discussed throughout the book, safe investments need to be balanced out with some good growth investments because over time, taxes and inflation can devastate your portfolio.

Just because you are retired doesn't mean that your tax bracket will automatically drop. Income from your investments may keep you in your preretirement tax bracket. And, again, you have to consider inflation. Even at a modest 4 percent inflation rate, your money will lose almost half its value over an eighteen-year period. After five years at 4 percent inflation, $100,000 will be worth $82,000; after ten years it will be worth $68,000; after fifteen years, $56,000. At the end of twenty years your $100,000 will be worth a paltry $46,000. Shocking, isn't it?

If you don't think you have a very good chance of seeing all of those twenty years, you're wrong. Currently, if you are age sixty-five, your life expectancy is approximately another twenty-one years. That's a long time to plan for. And a long time to have inflation eating away at your portfolio.

Why Bother? I've Lived My Life . . .

Just because you're sixtysomething and are approaching retirement or have already retired doesn't mean your life is over. You're not entering your "twilight years" or your "sunset years." Think of them as your golden years. The words *twilight* and *sunset* sound like you're close to comatose, but *golden*—that's another story, which is why this is a very important time in your life to be hands on with your money.

And guess what? Suddenly, being sixtysomething isn't "old" anymore. According to the U.S. Census Bureau, the number of Americans aged *fifty plus* has nearly doubled in the last fifty years, jumping from 33 million in 1933 to 63 million in 1992. By the year 2025, demographers predict that this segment of the population will number 113 million Americans.

In fact, the *sixty-five years and older group* is one of the fastest-growing segments of the population, expected to increase by one-third in the years 1980 to 2000. It is projected that this age group will comprise 13.1 percent of the population by the year 2000.

What all of these numbers add up to if you're a sixtysomething woman today is that you have a very good chance of living to age eighty, ninety, one hundred, and beyond. This means that your financial planning is far from over when you reach sixtysomething. In many ways you are beginning a completely new phase of your financial life. The big question is, will you have the income that you need to live the life-style that you want to live during your retirement years?

Retirement Myths and Realities

Somehow, we've all been programmed to believe that our retirement years will be the time in our lives when we will finally have a chance to relax and enjoy the good life. This is a lovely thought and a wonderful sentiment, but it is nothing more than a myth unless we prepare ourselves adequately. Consider the following retirement myths and realities:

Myth. Since I'm only fifty and I have a good fifteen years of work ahead of me, retirement isn't something I need to worry about now.

Reality. Ideally, everyone should begin retirement planning as soon as they get their first job. Statistics clearly indicate that as we move toward the year 2000, we'll be living longer and spending more years in retirement.

If you are age fifty with an annual income of $75,000, it's estimated that apart from your contributions to Social Security and retirement instruments like an IRA and 401(k) plan, you'll need to put aside an additional $4,000 a year every year until you retire in order to maintain your preretirement life-style.

Myth. Retirement means a decrease in my living expenses.

Reality. When you retire, you will have more free time for travel, leisure activities, hobbies, and other interests that you may want to pursue. All of this can add up to an increase in expenses.

In addition, medical expenses will increase at a faster rate than they did during your preretirement years. Medicare pays less than half of a retiree's medical bills. And you usually can't start collecting until age sixty-five. Also, many employers are cutting back on medical coverage for retirees because of the high cost, so make sure you're not left underinsured or, worse, uninsured.

Myth. My Social Security income will be more than adequate for my retirement needs.

Reality. You will need at least 75 to 80 percent of your annual preretirement income to maintain your standard of living once you retire. Social Security will probably provide less than half the amount that you need. And this amount may continue to decrease in the future.

Social Security accounted for 38 percent of the average retiree's income in 1990. That year the average benefit for all retirees was approximately $602 per month.

Myth. My pension plan will provide the additional funds that I need.

Reality. You may not get nearly the pension benefits that you expect:

> • Women retiring from jobs in the business world can expect smaller pensions than men. Because many women were late entrants to the workplace, they have fewer years to accumulate pension benefits.

> • Half of all workers have no pension plan at all.

> • During the 1980s more than two thousand corporations dipped into employee pension funds to the tune of at least $1 million each.

> • Those of you who work for local, state, and federal governments may consider yourselves underpaid, but you will probably receive larger pension benefits than those employed in the private sector.

Consider the following statistics regarding average annual pension benefits for 1990: retired federal worker = $12,966; retired state or local government worker = $9,068; retired private-sector worker = $6,512.

The private pension system is deteriorating, and it is becoming increasingly clear that the Social Security system will lack the financial resources to compensate for what we won't be getting from our private pensions.

Even if you do receive what's coming to you, nine out of ten pension plans are not indexed for inflation. To illustrate once again the erosion of purchasing power: If you are a sixty-five-year-old retiree getting a nonindexed pension benefit of $18,000 a year, in ten years your $18,000 will purchase only $12,000 worth of goods and services, applying the current inflation rate of 4 percent. In twenty years, using the same 4 percent inflation factor, your $18,000 pension will give you about $8,000 of actual purchasing power. This means that over a twenty-year period, at a mild 4 percent inflation, you've lost $10,000 worth of purchasing power.[6]

How Sixtysomething Can Be Comfortable *and* Profitable

Although it is likely that you will be shifting your portfolio toward more income-oriented investments, you *don't* want to move totally into income investments and totally out of growth investments. If you are seventy years old, it's very appropriate to have 70 percent of your money in income investments. But many investors, like Margaret, go to the extreme of keeping 100 percent of their money in income investments. Because of their age, they don't think that growth investments in general—and stocks in particular—are suitable for them. If this describes your investment approach, remember that *growing poor safely can be hazardous to your wealth.*

In today's low interest rate environment, to get the income you need you may want to consider owning some stocks. What's interesting to me is the number of investors who have "stock phobia." They would rather put their investment dollars in complicated high-yield products that are supposedly safe than look to well-managed stock mutual funds.

Historically, dollar for dollar, stocks have outperformed all other investments. From 1945 through 1991 stocks as represented by the S&P 500 returned an average of 11.8 percent. Small-company stocks did even better, returning 13.3 percent. Bonds, on the other hand, fared a lot less well. U.S. government bonds posted an average annual return of 4.8 percent; corporate bonds returned 5.4 percent.

According to a study done by Ibbotson Associates, Inc., a Chicago-based research firm, from 1926 through 1989 a hypothetical investment of $1 performed as follows:

$1 invested in the stock market . . . . grew to $534
$1 invested in government bonds . . . . grew to $17.30
$1 invested in T-bills . . . . grew to less than $10

Given the reality of inflation combined with this strong case for stock ownership, does this mean that you should fill your portfolio with nothing but stocks? Absolutely not. But it certainly doesn't make sense to leave them out altogether.

To structure a well-diversified income portfolio properly, consider using a mix of high-quality bonds, preferred stocks, utility stocks, and high-yield common stocks (not to be confused with high-yield junk bonds). For inflation protection—to hedge against the erosion of your purchasing power—you will need to include some growth stocks as well.

When in Doubt, Invest in Yourself

Some of you may be investing for the first time or be considering owning stocks for the first time. How to pick and choose? Again, it involves one of the consistent investment themes that you've read about throughout this book: the two Cs and two Ds, your common sense, comfort level, diversification, and discipline.

Use and apply what you observe in your everyday life. Don't go too far afield. Why not invest in yourself—in the goods and services that reflect the needs and interests of your own age group?

The travel and leisure industries, for example, stand to gain from affluent senior citizens, who will spend their retirement years— and their retirement dollars—traveling and enjoying leisure activities.

It is certainly true that many sixtysomething Americans lack the financial resources to live even comfortably in retirement. But others, including those who profited from investing in the recent bull market, managed to build sizable retirement nest eggs. Many investors also cashed in on the appreciation of one of the strongest real estate markets in history. Statistics indicate that our retired population is increasingly affluent.

And healthier. Sixtysomething Americans are not only living longer than previous generations, they're living healthier as good nutrition and exercise are becoming more and more a part of sixtysomething life. Of course, this doesn't eliminate the need for health care. So consider investing in pharmaceutical companies, health care providers, and other related industries that will benefit from the aging of America.

Since many retirees migrate to the Sunbelt—particularly to Florida and the Southwest—it also makes sense to invest in utility companies in these areas. Assuming that the sixtysomething population will continue to increase, it stands to reason that there will be substantial growth in the utility and energy sectors in these particular parts of the country.

Need Additional Monthly Income?

Utility stocks pay dividends quarterly, as do nearly all common and preferred stocks. But what if you need monthly income from your investments? How do you achieve this?

One solution is to invest in a "basket" of income stocks that pay dividends in different months. For example, you can invest in three different utility stocks paying dividends as follows:

Stock #1: pays dividends in January, April, July, October
Stock #2: pays dividends in February, May, August, November
Stock #3: pays dividends in March, June, September, December

This way you will have money coming in every month.

Likewise, if you choose to own individual bonds that pay interest semiannually, invest in six different bonds so that you're receiving interest income every month.

Another solution is to invest in a bond mutual fund that pays monthly income. You can have interest checks sent directly to you, or they can be deposited into your money market account.

Unit investment trusts pay monthly income as well. Like a bond mutual fund, they can be taxable, partially taxable, or completely tax-free. Unit investment trusts are essentially buy and hold mutual funds. The portfolio is well diversified, but the bonds are held to maturity, not traded like a mutual fund.

You may also want to consider investing in Ginnie Maes for monthly income. When you purchase a GNMA, you invest in a pool of mortgages issued by the Federal Housing Administration or the Veterans Administration. As the mortgage holders make their monthly payments, the money is "passed through" to you, the GNMA investor.

Although GNMAs are generally considered safe investments (the principal and interest on the loans are guaranteed by the U.S. government), remember that they are also self-amortizing. This means that your monthly income will include principal as well as interest.

Ginnie Maes have historically yielded about 1 percent more than long-term government bonds.

You Can't Take It with You

If the quality of your life depends on spending the income from your investments, by all means spend it. But if you want to preserve your estate for your heirs, you may not want to invade principal. And you may even choose to reinvest some of the income.

For many of you, ensuring that your heirs will benefit from your estate is more than a goal. It may be a major driving force in your life. I've known many sixtysomething women who grew up very poor and were determined that their children and grandchildren would never do without and never experience the financial pain that's about a lot more than an empty purse or wallet.

Estate planning is an important part of your financial planning. If you choose to make provisions for relatives and other loved ones, you'll want to do so in a way that minimizes potential tax liability. You obviously don't want your gift to be consumed by excessive taxation.

Here are a few tips to get you started in the right direction:

- If you die without a will, more than half of your estate will go to the government to pay taxes.

- You can escape the capital gains tax by keeping your securities, real estate, and other appreciated assets until you die. Your heirs are likely to pay less taxes when these investments are sold than you would have paid had you sold them during your lifetime.

- The marital exemption allows you to make unlimited bequests to your spouse *estate tax free.*

- A living trust, unlike a will, bypasses probate. Think of a living trust as a house. All of your financial assets are the furniture in this house. It protects your assets from the lengthy and costly probate system, which can take anywhere from six months to several years. This house or living trust, properly structured, can significantly reduce estate taxes and greatly speed up the distribution of assets.

Be sure to consult with a top-notch estate planning attorney for help in structuring the best estate plan for you. Spending money to get expert legal advice now can save your heirs substantial money—and hassle—later.

The Gift That Keeps on Giving

You may also want to talk to an estate-planning attorney about the best way to make lifetime gifts. By doing this, you can substantially reduce your heirs' estate taxes. And you get to enjoy watching your loved ones enjoy your gift.

Any one person can gift to another person a maximum of $10,000 each year without incurring any gift tax liability. A husband and wife are allowed to gift $20,000 to any one person each year. If you have five grandchildren, you and your husband together can potentially gift to them up to $100,000 a year tax free.

Buying that first home or paying for a college education is a lot tougher today than it was forty and fifty years ago. Helping your loved ones while you're still alive is like playing fairy godmother. You get to watch their dreams come true!

Retirement and Your Life-style Decisions

Life-style decisions are your most important decisions for your retirement years. Your money is what you use to facilitate them. How you spend your time—starting a volunteer program at your local community center, developing an interest in photography, exploring eighteenth-century castles in Europe—should not be dictated by what you can afford, but rather by what you choose to do.

If you have a comfortable retirement because you planned it early on, don't think the planning stops now. You need to continue to monitor your money and, if necessary, alter your investment strategy so you can live the life you choose.

You have goals during your retirement years. Why should this time of your life be different from any other? You had goals during your twentysomething years and during your fortysomething years. Your retirement years aren't any less important than other times in your life.

Your perception of this part of your life will greatly influence how you manage your retirement money. People who view this as "the beginning of the end" often become miserly and fearful. Rather than embrace life and live it for all it's worth, they retreat from life and start hoarding money.

They can literally make themselves sick with worry as they watch inflation consume what's left of their money. It's the ultimate self-fulfilling prophecy.

Growing poor safely can be hazardous to your wealth—and definitely does little for your health.

If you remember the statistics about life expectancy, when you reach sixty-five the first thought that should cross your mind is not How much time do I have left? Instead, it should be, How do I choose to spend the next twenty to thirty years of my life?

Let me share with you a lovely story about a woman named Laura.

Unfortunately, Laura was widowed at an early age, and she never remarried.

A mother of three, Laura worked as a secretary. This was during a time when few women worked outside the home. Says Laura, "I had to climb three flights of stairs to get to the ladies' room. They didn't have a restroom on every floor for women as they did for men."

When Laura retired at age sixty-five, she was well compensated by her company for her thirty-seven years of devotion and hard work. During her career, happily, she had watched her three children grow up, go to college, and start their own families. Her dreams had come true. All except for one.

So instead of retiring to a recliner in front of the television set, Laura made a five-year goal. She loved to paint and appreciated all types of art. Laura was determined that by the time she reached seventy she would own her own art gallery.

This meant that she would have to shift some of her income investments into growth investments. She would have to sacrifice some safety and take some risk. But she studied the financial markets and asked lots of questions. By doing this, she felt comfortable with each investment decision that she made. And since she had a five-year goal, she employed a great deal of patience and discipline to ride out the ups and downs of some of her investments.

Laura spent her time painting, going to museums, enjoying her grandchildren, and keeping track of her money. Two weeks before her seventieth birthday, Laura opened a very special art gallery for other would-be artists called From the Heart. The only "credential" that artists needed to have their work shown was to be at least sixty-five!

Like Laura, most were painters who, due to life circumstances, had never been able to pursue their passion for art. The gallery provided them with a long overdue opportunity—and long overdue recognition. From the Heart also proved to be quite profitable and gave Laura not only years of pleasure, but the resources to provide young artists with scholarship money to pursue their dreams.

Her daughter took over running From the Heart when Laura turned eighty-five. But Laura continued to paint in the back room and inspire other artists for the rest of her life.

Always use the one-year Treasury bill as a benchmark for safety. This will help you gauge the risk potential of alternative investments. Unless you have a particular affinity for Florida swampland or don't mind being one of the multiple owners of the Brooklyn Bridge, steer clear of any investment that promises a higher return than you feel it should reasonably deliver.

Secret #11 . . .

If It Sounds Too Good to Be True, It Probably Is: Taking Care of Your Future

True story: Kathy Whitworth is a golfing legend. In fact, she is the most honored player in LPGA history. She joined the LPGA in 1959 and, over the years, broke all records with her total of eighty-eight official tour victories. She's won more tournaments than Sam Snead, Jack Nicklaus, Arnold Palmer, and every other big-time pro.

Did she make money? You bet. During her thirty-three-year career, she was the LPGA tour's top money winner eight times and earned more than $1.7 million.

Now, close to sixty and at an age when her fellow golfers are comfortably retired, Kathy is struggling to make a living by playing in pro ams, exhibitions—anything that will earn her money in the world of golf.

Why? Because she's still trying to replace the retirement money that she lost in 1981 when she transferred her total savings of $388,000 to a financial management company in San Jose, California. By 1986 the company's president and founder had been accused of mismanagement and fraud. Shortly after that the company defaulted on loan obligations, filed for reorganization under Chapter 11, and eventually folded. And along with the management company went nearly all of Kathy's retirement money.

Although a tough opponent on the links, Kathy was a sucker for a financial "sure thing." Through a friend she was introduced to the president of the management company, who was also a lawyer. He promised her that he would make her a fortune, risk free. Kathy believed him. She was also told that if any of her investments started losing money, the management company would buy the investments back from her.

Says Kathy, "It was all in writing and I thought, How can I lose?"

Because Kathy's friend had recommended this man and his company, she didn't bother to check out his credentials. And to Kathy, the nice, helpful people that she met at the management company were another indication that it was all legitimate. It seemed too good to be true . . . and in the end it was.

Kathy was able to recover about $150,000 from her "too good to be true" investment. Now, the money that she has and is able to earn is invested in blue-chip stocks and government-guaranteed securities.

Kathy's financial disaster stands out because she's a celebrity[7]—not because her story is so unusual. In fact, what happened to Kathy happens to older women all the time. Especially widows.

Sweet, kind, and trusting—older women are victims waiting to happen. They don't realize that *if it sounds too good to be true, it probably is.* And they don't have the self-confidence to believe that they are perfectly capable of learning about their finances. And taking charge of their money.

When Your Husband Says "I Do," It May Not Be Forever

Your husband's promise—"Don't worry, honey. I'll take care of you forever"—is the first *if it sounds too good to be true. . . .* It's a lovely sentiment, but unfortunately the statistics contradict him. Let me remind you that 75 percent of all married women outlive their husbands.

If you don't believe in statistics, consider the empirical evidence. Look at the number of women in retirement homes as compared to men. If you're sixtysomething, how many of your friends are women and how many are men? And if you're seventysomething . . . eightysomething . . . ?

When I was a little girl, I remember my grandma playing cards every Sunday. Poker was her game, and it was a nickel pot. I used to go over to her house and help her set up the tables and chairs and put out little dishes of mints and chocolate-covered raisins.

When I was five, all the card players were couples. By the time I reached my sweet sixteen, the men were few and far between and most of the players were women. And by the time I was in my mid-twenties, there were only two men left. The rest of the card players were widows. That's when I realized that women live longer than men. It was a pretty graphic lesson.

In retrospect, I wonder how many of Grandma's widowed girl-friends had their money houses in order? I wonder how many were being snookered out of the money their husbands had left them by smooth-talking hucksters out to make a quick buck at their expense. Many woman of their generation believed their husbands when they told them they would take care of them forever. Many of these women never learned to take care of themselves.

When your husband promises you that he'll take care of you for-ever, in his heart I'm sure he believes it and means it. Most of us don't have a true sense of our own mortality. This is why some husbands don't see the necessity of educating their wives financially. They be-lieve that they'll be the exception to the statistics. Besides, who wants to think about death?

Husbands don't like dealing with their mortality, and wives don't like thinking about ending up alone. It's easy to understand why peo-ple don't want to deal with these issues—they're just too difficult to deal with.

To me, the ultimate gift of love and caring is for your husband to include you financially, not take care of you. This means that he should sit down with you and make a list of all your assets, explain where everything is located, and introduce you to every "A-team" member with whom he has been working. The bottom line is that you have to be financially prepared should you outlive your husband. *Before you actually do outlive your husband.*

Ideally, this financial sharing should have begun the day you got married—but times were different then. But just because you're sixtysomething doesn't mean you can't learn now.

Unfortunately, too many sixtysomething women resist taking that first step into their financial lives. They don't want to learn something new. They don't want the responsibility. And they are convinced they can't do it. They tell me, "I've never dealt with money in my life—

except what my husband gave me to spend. And of course I've managed the household budget. But I'm close to seventy and I'm supposed to learn all of this now? Where would I start?" They don't realize that budgeting the household finances has shown them to be excellent money managers and prepared them very well for the money world at large.

Add to this the fact that sixtysomething women were raised in an era when even talking about money was unladylike and definitely less than proper. Is it any wonder that when their husbands pass away, they are relieved to turn over their financial affairs to some other man to take care of? These are the women who are ripe for victimization.

Could it happen to you?

Next Victim, Please

The world is full of unscrupulous people, and they come in all shapes, sizes, and professions. They pass themselves off as CPAs, stockbrokers, attorneys, business managers, money managers—you name it.

What these people really are are vultures. In this case their prey is older women: vulnerable, lonely, and usually lacking in financial self-confidence.

Believe it or not, these people actually shop the "widow market." They read the obituaries, looking for wealthy women recently widowed. Next victim, please. . . .

I saw a perfect example of this acted out on the television show "Taxi" several years ago. All the drivers at the cab company decide they're going to try "real" jobs. Louie De Palma (played by Danny De Vito) decides to be a stockbroker. There's an absolutely classic scene where Louie is shown talking on the phone to a hot prospect: "Oh, it's not a good time, Mrs. Baker? Would after the funeral be better?"

Danny De Vito's portrayal of loathsome Louie De Palma may be a caricature, but Louie exists. He's out there today, possibly wearing an Armani suit and a boyish grin—but he's out there.

With your husband gone—especially if he handled all of the finances—a tremendous fear takes over. Since you've always been taken care of, you are anxious to pass on the stewardship of your financial life to someone else who will relieve you of the anxiety and stress of having to handle something you know nothing about—your money. You want so much to trust *someone* because right now your grief is so all-consuming that you can't bear any additional responsibility. You're anxious just to have everything taken care of. That's understandable. But, ultimately, this can lead to financial disaster.

Suddenly, out of nowhere, you're surrounded by strangers saying, "Don't worry, I'll take care of you. I know your husband always took care of things. Well, now I'm going to do it. Don't give it another thought. You'll be well looked after. . . ." These can be the most comforting words in the world to a widow. But remember, *if it sounds too good to be true, it probably is.* The reality is that most of these "concerned" people couldn't care less about you. The only concern they have is for themselves—and lining their wallets with your money.

I've heard stories about women who have given these vultures power of attorney, which means they then had financial carte blanche. Once this occurs, anything can happen, from wildly inappropriate investments to out-and-out embezzlement. Many of these women can't afford risk. Yet they take the biggest risk of all by not completely checking out the person who is about to take over their financial life. They're buying temporary (and imaginary) peace of mind at a very high price.

Unfortunately, I've known several widows who have fallen prey to these smooth talkers. So if a Mr. Too Good to Be True suddenly enters your life, promising to take care of everything, screen him as you would any potential "A-team" member. Get references and talk to some of his clients. Ask him questions. If he tries to talk over your head, your antennae should go up immediately. It's a clear early-warning signal.

If he tries to make you feel inept by talking down to you, don't start doubting yourself. And don't back down. Older women get talked out of their warm fuzzies more quickly than anyone. They rationalize, "Well, I'm getting on, and he's a lot younger and smarter than I am. He knows what's going on in the world, and he knows about money. . . ."

Don't become a victim just because you're vulnerable. When you've suffered a loss, it's extremely tempting to shortcut the interviewing process, even to skip getting references. All you want to do is pull down the shades and close out the world so you can be left alone to work through your grief.

But you know that business still must be taken care of, and since you're not up to it, why not pass the buck (literally) to someone who is more than willing to deal with it? If you do this, by the time you finally lift the shades and are ready to live again, you may discover that you have very little left to live on.

Money lost at this point in your life will be difficult to replace. You may not have the earning potential that you had when you were younger. And if you've never worked outside your home, you may not want to start now. *Why be forced to?*

Friendly Family

The most subtle victimization, often the most difficult to detect, can be by family members. All of a sudden you're the rich relative and everyone wants to be your best friend. They want to help you, to do things for you . . . and, oh, by the way, they need a loan.

I have a very sharp seventysomething client who told me what she thought was a funny story. It's a story that illustrates exactly the kind of victimization I'm talking about.

After Bernice's husband died, her granddaughter Marisa started showing up to run errrands and take her to the hairdresser. It was, "Oh, Grandma, what do you need at the market? Grandma, would you like me to come by and take you to a movie?" What amused Bernice was that she and Marisa had never been particularly close. She had always thought Marisa was nice—but they had never really connected.

Bernice saw right through this sudden concern for her well-being. She told me, "I'm convinced that Marisa thinks that by becoming my best friend I'll leave her all my money. Well, I'm leaving the exact same amount to each of my six grandchildren. But I don't tell any of them that because this way *everybody* can try to be my best friend. But nobody's going to get more money. I'm a very fair person."

Bernice was smart. She could have told her granddaughter, "Look, Marisa, you're not going to get any more than any of the other grandchildren." Instead she let Marisa do for her and cater to her, running herself ragged in the hope of getting the lion's share of the money.

Bernice played it for everything it was worth. She got lots of attention and had all of her needs met. Here was Marisa running errands all over town, thinking by doing this she would ace out all the other grandchildren.

Bernice's attitude was, "Great! Let her do all of these wonderful things for me. I'm giving everybody the same money anyway."

But she never told Marisa this because she knew that all the attention probably would stop. Said Bernice, "I'm finally getting to know my granddaughter, and even though I can see right through her, I like her, and she tickles me no end."

There are ways to play your older years to the hilt. Let everyone knock themselves out trying to please you. But the bottom line is to understand when people are being genuine and when you're being manipulated. If you can answer yes to any of the following questions, be on guard:

- Are people suddenly going out of their way to be nice to you?

- Are they asking questions about your financial life?

- Are they offering to do your banking for you?

- Are they making suggestions on how you can cut down on your expenses?

- Have you been asked to sign any papers that you don't understand?

This kind of stuff goes on all the time. Don't be an accident waiting to happen.

What? Me Manipulated?

If you have stayed single all your life, you probably take a great deal of pride in your financial independence. And if you have managed your money wisely, you've also probably amassed quite a tidy nest egg.

That's certainly true of my neighbor Lynette. But, as Lynette tells it, there is a strange kind of guilt that can set in, making her feel uncomfortable about having so much when those around her have so little: "There's the fellow who delivers my groceries. He wears sneakers full of holes. And the gardener who brings his little twins to visit me. I feel so sorry for them," she says.

I know Lynette's gardener because he used to work for me. He's a real smart cookie, that one. While Lynette's feeling sorry for him, he's probably trying to figure out a way to become her heir, without seeming apparent. If you're single and sixtysomething, people think of you as a rich woman with no one to leave your money to, so they cozy up to you and try to get on your good side. After all, you have to leave your money to someone, don't you?

Romeo, Romeo

Always be wary of sudden love interests on your romantic horizon. We've all heard about sixtysomething women being courted by thirtysomething boyfriends with romance on their lips and larceny in their hearts. If you do fall in love when you're sixtysomething, just make sure it's *real* for both of you. If it is, good for you! But if your new honey acts hurt because you don't want to fund a joint checking account, he's probably looking for more than love.

You deserve to be loved, and you deserve to be treated well. But emotional manipulation isn't love, and you don't have to tolerate it.

Charity Begins at Home

Don't be surprised if you are also courted by lots of charities. Many charities solicit contributions from older people, particularly single, sixtysomething women. It's wonderful to donate money, but make sure that the charity is legitimate and the cause is one you believe in. Sad to say, there are plenty of scam artists out there masquerading as representatives of charitable organizations. So be generous, if you wish, to those who deserve it—but dubious of those who don't.

Older and Wiser

Why do some people assume that when you get older, you suddenly become brain dead? Getting older does *not* mean that you automatically become feebleminded. Unless you really are sick, quite the opposite is true. You're *older and wiser*. You've lived through so much and have experienced the highs and lows of life. If you compare yourself with those around you, chances are good that you're the most together, most sensible person in your family.

So how come some of those same people start treating you like a cute little Cabbage Patch doll or as if you don't have a mind? Do you know how many people live to be one hundred and then some, living full, active lives? The U.S. Census Bureau counted 35,808 people one hundred years and older in 1990. This is double what it was in 1980. It's expected that by the year 2080 at least one million people will live to be one hundred and older.

Turning sixtysomething could very well be the beginning of a whole new life, a wonderful time of life. Unfortunately, older people aren't exactly venerated in this country, as we all know. They are victimized and neglected. There are horror stories about Grandma and Grandpa dumping, in which people who don't want to care for their elderly parents drop them off at a shopping mall and just leave them there. Charming, isn't it?

The P.S. to all of this is that the sixtysomething woman owes it to herself to take care of herself. Whether you're single, divorced, married, or widowed, recognize the fact that you are your own responsibility. It's rare to find someone who puts your best interest first—even your husband.

So stay on your toes and don't let anyone victimize you. Let them curry favor, run errands, whatever—as long as you know that you are still controlling the bucks. The buck stops with you—or wherever you say it does.

Whether you want to be very hands on about managing your money or choose to work with a professional money manager, always maintain control. And always have reasonable expectations about investment performance.

Remember to use the one-year Treasury bill as a benchmark for safety. This will help you gauge the risk potential of alternative investments. Be realistic. If one-year Treasuries are yielding 4 percent, be wary of "too good to be true" promises of higher yield without higher risk. Anything that claims "15 percent, risk free" is improbable at best, fraudulent at worst. Likewise are many second trust deeds, "safe" private loans, and, certainly, almost all get-rich-quick schemes involving options and commodities trading.

Unless you have a particular affinity for Florida swampland or don't mind being one of the multiple owners of the Brooklyn Bridge, steer clear of any investment that promises a higher return than you feel it should reasonably deliver.

You won't get victimized unless you believe in things that you shouldn't believe in. You can also become a victim if you trust people you shouldn't trust or if you're too quick to trust because you *need* to trust. When in doubt, apply your common sense and always trust your warm fuzzies.

It's up to you to be cautious and not to be so trusting or so quick to believe. Again, it all goes back to the two Cs and two Ds. Use your common sense, don't agree to anything that makes you uncomfortable, use diversification by never relying too heavily on any one person, and have the discipline to say no when it's in your own best interest.

If It Sounds Too Good to Be True, It Probably Is

If you believe in things that sound too good to be true, then you are a victim waiting to happen. But if you trust your instincts, ask the right questions, and understand that you can *and should* take care of yourself, your sixtysomething years can be your best years.

And that *is* true!

 Money is power. Taking control of your financial life is, bottom line, an empowering experience that has an enormous up side and no down side. It feels great and is very much its own reward.

Conclusion . . .
Where Do We Go from Here?

You now know the money secrets. The world of money has become accessible. You've learned the language and the basic strategies. And you know the pitfalls.

The door is open, so step in!

Don't wait until next January 1 to make—*and keep*—these twelve money resolutions:

1. Start putting your money house in order now. And stop waiting for someone else to do it for you magically. Elves show up only at Christmastime, and they seldom stick around to balance your checkbook.

2. Get a handle on your income and your outgo, and where the twain don't meet. If you're not sure where your money goes each month, find out. Break down your expenses for the last six months. It's relatively painless and shouldn't take more than two hours. It will be time well spent.

3. Pay off credit card debt ASAP. It doesn't make sense to borrow at a whopping 18 to 22 percent, especially since the interest isn't even deductible anymore. If you have money in a savings or money market account, use it to pay down your debt. It's probably earning you less than 4 percent in the bank, and it's costing you more than quadruple that to borrow on your credit cards.

4. Save for tomorrow today even if you're light-years away from retirement. Your child may be a newborn, but she'll be off to college before you can hum "Sunrise, Sunset." Set up a separate savings account and pay it like a bill every month before you pay your other bills—not just if there's money left over. If you can't save much, save what you can. Start small, but start.

5. Make a money plan and stick to it. As in life, failing to plan is planning to fail. Saving, spending, and investing should all work together instead of in a vacuum. A good solid financial plan is the blueprint for building financial security and future wealth.

6. Be realistic. If you try to get rich quick, you may get poor even quicker. Your financial goals should have some stretch in them, but it's important to have reasonable expectations. It's hard to retire at fifty-five if you don't start saving until you're fifty.

7. Do you know where your money is? If you have multiple bank accounts, brokerage accounts, mutual funds, and retirement plans, keeping up to date on your investments can be a primal scream experience. Consolidate accounts where it makes sense and review your statements at least quarterly. It's time to take stock of where your money is and how hard it's working for you.

8. Educate yourself. There is nothing very mysterious about money. Most women just don't speak the language. Bankerspeak and brokerese can make investing inaccessible. Learn the lingo and get the big picture by asking questions, reading, taking classes, and tuning in to business shows on television and radio.

9. Assemble your "A team." Put together a top-notch group of advisers, including your banker, broker or certified financial planner, CPA, and attorney. Make sure that you're comfortable talking to them and that they're comfortable talking to each other. If you're not happy with the ability or attitude of one of your advisers, find a new one. A relationship that doesn't work doesn't have to be 'til death do you part.

10. Take the long view. Don't let your money plan be derailed by the day-to-day vagaries of the markets, or you'll never arrive at your financial destination on time and in one piece. If making a change is warranted, fine. But if it ain't broke, don't fix it.

11. Get back to the basics. The go-go days of the 1980s are over. The two Cs and two Ds—common sense, comfort level, diversification, and discipline—are the watchwords of the 1990s. In simple English: Do what makes sense, do what feels right, don't put all your eggs in one basket, and don't be greedy. An old Wall Street aphorism has it that bulls and bears make money. Pigs get slaughtered.

12. Understand that money is power. Taking control of your financial life is, bottom line, an empowering experience that has an enormous up side and no down side. It feels great and is very much its own reward.

To be sure, money is a complex, confusing issue. However, when women look at the financial arena, we know we can understand it. We've conquered so much in the last several decades, accomplished goals we thought were impossible to achieve. Dealing with money is just another frontier.

SOURCES

1. Internal Revenue Service (based on 1988 figures).
2. Bureau of Labor Statistics.
3. Oppenheimer Management Corporation.
4. National Foundation for Women Business Owners.
5. U.S. House of Representatives Committee on Small Business.
6. "Retirement Myths and Realities" adapted from "The Myths and Realities of Retirement Planning," *American Association of Individual Investors Journal,* September 1991.
7. Kathy Whitworth story taken from "Playing out of Deep Rough," *Sports Illustrated,* September 30, 1991.

About the Author

Esther M. Berger is a certified financial planner and first vice president of PaineWebber Incorporated, Beverly Hills. Her interest in women's issues has made her especially sensitive to the needs of her female clients, including single and married women, divorcees, and widows. She uses her professional expertise to help women overcome their fears about money and determine their own financial futures.

She is a frequent speaker to business and professional groups as well as to philanthropic organizations. In 1991, at the invitation of the Pentagon, she addressed its Senior Professional Women's Association, which meets under the auspices of the secretary of defense. Ms. Berger has been published in *Newsweek*'s "My Turn" and has been interviewed by CNN, *USA Today, The New York Times, Los Angeles Times, Lear's, Savvy, Money, Worth, Self, Success, Working Woman,* Financial News Network, and News Limited Australia. Ms. Berger is a columnist for *Experience,* the magazine of the senior lawyers' division of the American Bar Association, and for the *Women's Information News Service,* a publication of the Divorced and Widowed Women's Network.

She lives in Beverly Hills with her husband, Leo, a certified public accountant, and their three sons.